# Childcraft

## THE HOW AND WHY LIBRARY

### VOLUME 7

# Story of the Sea

**World Book, Inc.**

a Scott Fetzer company

Chicago   London   Sydney   Toronto

World Book, Inc.
525 W. Monroe
Chicago, IL 60661

ISBN 0-7166-0194-x
Library of Congress Catalog Card Number 93-60976
Printed in the United States of America
A/ID

# Acknowledgments

The publishers of *Childcraft—The How and Why
Library* gratefully acknowledge the courtesy of
the following publishers, agencies, authors, and
organizations for permission to use copyrighted
material in this volume. Full illustration
acknowledgments appear on page 280.

Macmillan, London and Basingstoke: "The Starfish" by
Carmen Bernos DeGasztold, from *Beasts' Choir* by Carmen
Bernos DeGasztold. Reprinted by permission of Macmillan,
London and Basingstoke.

Macmillan Publishing Co., Inc.: Excerpts from "Sea-Fever"
by John Masefield, reprinted with permission of Macmillan
Publishing Co., Inc., from *Poems* by John Masefield.

Oxford University Press: Excerpt from *Beowulf,* translated
by Charles Kennedy, reprinted by permission of Oxford
University Press.

The Society of Authors: Excerpts from "Sea-Fever" by
John Masefield, reprinted by permission of The Society
of Authors as the literary representatives of the
Estate of John Masefield.

Viking Penguin, Inc.: "The Starfish" by Carmen Bernos
DeGasztold, from *The Creatures' Choir* by Carmen Bernos
DeGasztold. Translated from the French by Rumer Godden.
Copyright © Rumer Godden 1965. All rights reserved.
Reprinted by permission of Viking Penguin, Inc.

Volume 7

# Story of the Sea

## Contents

# Introduction

Have you ever stood on a beach and looked out to sea? The water stretches on and on until it appears to join the sky! It hardly seems possible that anything could be so big! But the sea *is* big. There is three times more water than there is land.

On a calm, sunny day, the sea seems bright and happy. On a cloudy, windy day, it seems dark and restless. In a storm, it is angry and fierce. The sea has many moods.

As you look out to sea, you may, if you're lucky, spot the dark streak of a whale's back, or the fin of a shark. Most of the time, the sea seems to be just a great, empty expanse of water. It's hard to imagine that it's actually the home of billions of creatures.

You may see a ship. Perhaps it's a fishing vessel setting out to make its catch, for the sea is an important source of food. Or you may see a merchant ship carrying a cargo from a faraway land. The sea has been a "highway" for ships for thousands of years.

Perhaps, as you stare at the sea, you'll think of some of the stories you've heard: of sea monsters and mermaids, ghost ships and pirates, sea battles and explorers. For the sea is a place of mystery and adventure.

The sea itself is a story. It is the story of discovery and commerce, exploration and adventure. It is the story of strange animals and their ways. It is the story of people who have challenged the sea, who have made it their work and their way of life.

This book is the story of the sea.

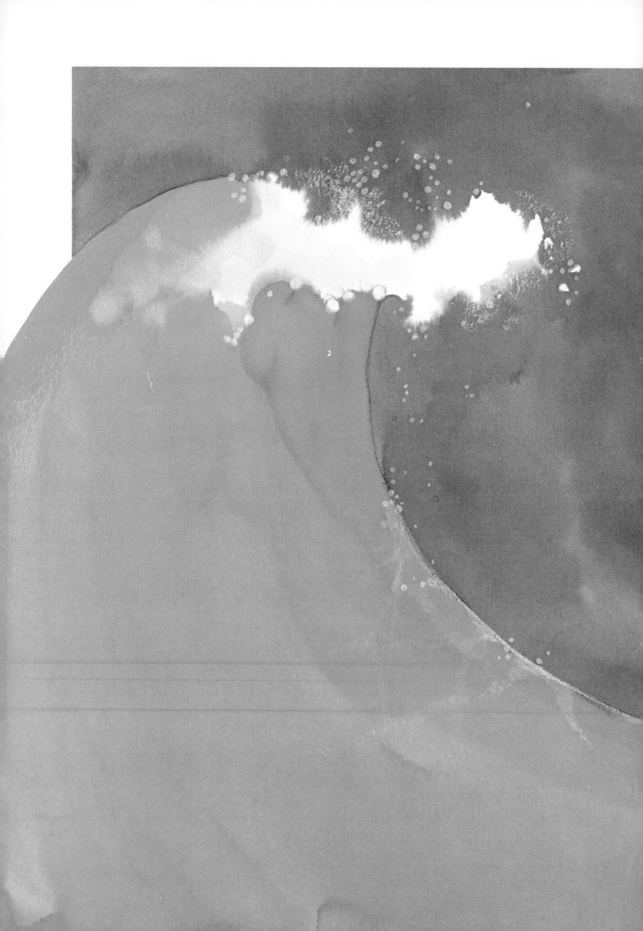

# Might and majesty of the sea

The rain is raining all around,
  It falls on field and tree,
It rains on the umbrellas here,
  And on the ships at sea.

*Rain*
by Robert Louis Stevenson

Of speckled eggs the birdie sings
  And nests among the trees;
The sailor sings of ropes and things
  In ships upon the seas.

The children sing in far Japan,
  The children sing in Spain;
The organ with the organ man
  Is singing in the rain.

*Singing*
by Robert Louis Stevenson

9

I saw a ship a-sailing,
    A-sailing on the sea,
And oh but it was laden
    With pretty things for me.

Mother Goose

Little drops of water,
    Little grains of sand,
Make the mighty ocean
    And the pleasant land.

Mother Goose

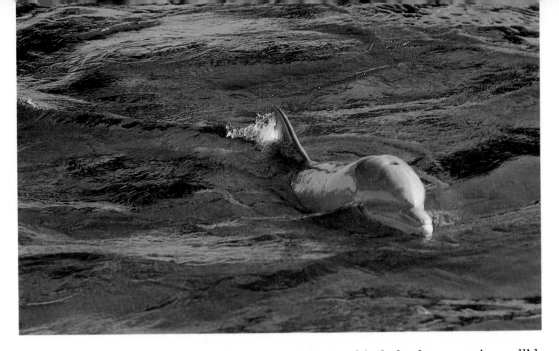

. . . the whale it whistled, the porpoise roll'd,
And the dolphins bared their backs of gold.

from *The Sea*
by Barry Cornwall

I spread my star-points wide
and dream, dream, dream . . . .
Lord,
an angel
could root me up
from the bottom of the sea
and set me back
in Your sky.
Oh! One day
could that be?
      Amen.

from *The Starfish*
by Carmen Bernos de Gasztold
Translated from the French
by Rumer Godden

Sea Shell, Sea Shell,
   Sing me a song, O please!
A song of ships, and sailormen,
   And parrots, and tropical trees,

Of islands lost in the Spanish Main
Which no man ever may find again,
Of fishes and corals under the waves,
And sea horses stabled in great green caves.

Sea Shell, Sea Shell,
Sing of the things you know so well.

*Sea Shell*
by Amy Lowell

And like the wings of sea-birds
Flash the white caps of the sea

from *Twilight*
by Henry Wadsworth Longfellow

I must go down to the seas again,
    for the call of the running tide
Is a wild call and a clear call
    that may not be denied.

from *Sea-Fever*
by John Masefield

Where shall we adventure, to-day that we're afloat,
    Wary of the weather and steering by a star?
Shall it be to Africa, a-steering of the boat,
    To Providence, or Babylon, or off to Malabar?

from *Pirate Story*
by Robert Louis Stevenson

Now the great winds shoreward blow,
Now the salt tides seaward flow;
Now the wild white horses play,
Champ and chafe and toss in the spray.

from *The Forsaken Merman*
by Matthew Arnold

When I was down beside the sea
A wooden spade they gave to me
   To dig the sandy shore.
My holes were empty like a cup,
In every hole the sea came up,
   Till it could come no more.

*At the Seaside*
by Robert Louis Stevenson

23

# Water world

# The wonder of water

The sea is, of course, water—the stuff we
drink, wash in, cook with, and swim in, and
the stuff that falls from the sky when it
rains. Water is so common we take it for
granted. But it's actually one of the most
amazing—and perhaps one of the most rare—

materials in the whole universe. Without it, there would be no life on earth. So far as we know, without water there can't be any life anywhere.

Scientists think that life on earth began in the sea. The first living things were made mostly of water. And it is a fact that every living thing now on earth is made mostly of water. It is also a fact that the body fluids in people and animals are almost exactly the same as seawater. The reason plants and animals take in water is to keep the same amount of water in their bodies at all times. If a living creature does not have enough water in its body, it will soon die.

But just what *is* water? Water is a liquid made out of two gases! Air is made of gases, so you know that gas is dry, "thin" stuff that you can't see or feel. But when two gases, oxygen and hydrogen, mix together in a certain way, they become wet, weighty water!

Water is the only substance on earth that can be found in three different forms. It can be a liquid, as it is in the ocean. It can be a solid, as it is when it is ice. And it can be a gas, as it is when it is steam or the water vapor of a cloud.

Water is a powerful chemical. You can put many kinds of strong, tough metals into it and, in time, it will dissolve them.

Water is certainly wonderful, almost magical stuff, as well as the very material of life itself. And scientists think that water may be quite rare. There is none on any of the other planets that we know about. Perhaps the great sea that covers much of our planet is a very unusual thing.

# The gift from the sea

Without the sea, there would be no life on the land.

Snow, piled up on mountaintops, melts and trickles down mountainsides to become rivers. Rain and snow that fall to earth soak into the ground and provide moisture that plants must have for life. Thus, without rain and snow there would be no fresh water and no plants. Without fresh water to drink and plants to eat, there would be no animals.

And most of the rain and snow that make life possible, come from the *sea*.

The heat of the sun causes a great deal of the water on the surface of the sea to evaporate, or become a gas. This gas—water vapor—rises into the air and forms the clouds we see in the sky. Wind carries the clouds over the land. When the clouds move into cooler air, the water vapor turns back into droplets of water that fall as rain or snow.

Thus, a soft summer rain, or a fierce winter blizzard, actually begins in the waters of the sea. And this rain and snow—the gift from the sea—make life on land possible.

The sea also makes life more comfortable for many of the creatures that live on land. For the sea controls the earth's climate.

There is much more water than land, and the temperature of water changes more slowly than that of land. So, the ocean helps keep the temperature of the air fairly steady. If there were no sea, the air around most of the earth would be very hot during the day, even in winter. And nights would be freezing cold, even in summer.

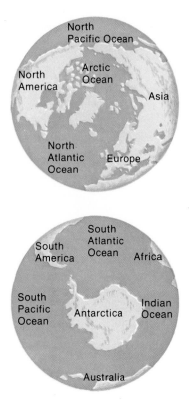

Look at a globe from the top or the bottom. You will see that all the oceans are really joined to one another and form a single body of water.

# The world ocean

More than three-quarters of our world is covered with water. Most of this water forms what we call the ocean. Although we have given special names to parts of the ocean, it is actually *one* huge body of water. The earth's continents are simply big "islands" surrounded by the water of this one world ocean.

The part of the ocean that lies between North and South America and Europe and Africa is called the Atlantic Ocean. The part that's between North and South America and Asia is called the Pacific Ocean. The part between Africa and Australia, and south of India, is the Indian Ocean. There is an Arctic Ocean at the top of the world. And the waters at the bottom of the world are sometimes called the Antarctic Ocean. All of these "oceans" are really connected to each other.

The ocean is often called the sea. And people sometimes speak of "the seven seas." But the word *sea* really means a body of water that is smaller than an ocean, or part of an ocean—such as the Mediterranean Sea. Even so, whether we call it "the ocean" or "the sea," we really mean that single great body of water that covers three-quarters of the earth's surface.

The ocean is warm in some places and cold in others. It is filled with dissolved minerals of all kinds, especially salt. And it is the home of a huge number of animals of all kinds—from some of the tiniest of all creatures to the very biggest that have ever lived.

# The birth of the sea

The sea may have been formed by tremendous rains. Or, it may have been formed by steam from inside the earth.

Scientists think the earth was formed more than four and one-half billion years ago. There was no water on its surface for a long time. Its inside was so hot that it was a liquid, as much of it still is today. Its outside, too, was probably so frightfully hot that a drop of water touching it would simply have sizzled at once into steam.

Slowly, the outside of the earth cooled off. Some scientists think that when the earth cooled enough, water vapor in the atmosphere changed into water and fell to earth as rain. Such a great rain would have lasted a very long time. Gradually, all the low parts of the surface would have filled up with water.

Other scientists think that as the earth's surface cooled, steam came rushing up out of volcanoes and geysers, just as it does today. When the steam hit the cool air, it was changed into water. The water then ran downhill. Slowly, over millions of years, it filled up the lowest parts of earth's rocky crust.

So, we don't know *exactly* how the sea was formed. But from what scientists have learned about the earth's rocks and its chemistry, they think the sea must have been formed in one of these two ways—or, perhaps, in a combination of both ways.

# The bottom of the sea

Have you ever wondered what's at the bottom of the sea? Well, it's land, of course.

When the sea was formed, water filled the low parts of the earth and covered much of the land. So, there is land beneath the sea. This land is much like the land above the sea.

However, the land beneath the sea is really *grander* than that above! Beneath the sea are ranges of mountains that are longer and wider than any mountain ranges on land. There are longer, deeper valleys, too. In the Pacific Ocean there are many great valleys in the ocean floor. The water in some valleys is so deep that if Mount Everest, the highest mountain on land, were put into one of them, its top would be more than a mile below the surface!

There are volcanoes on the sea bottom, too. Sometimes these volcanoes erupt, pouring out tons of red-hot, liquid rock that makes the water boil. As the liquid rock cools and grows solid, it makes the volcano taller. Many of the underwater volcanoes have grown so high that they stick up out of the water. We call the part that sticks out an island. The Hawaiian Islands are really the tops of huge underwater volcanoes.

All of the broad plains and deep valleys of the ocean floor are covered with layers of mud. In most places the mud is hundreds of feet (meters) deep. This mud has been building up for millions of years. It is made up of bits of sand, clay, and other material that has drifted down from the surface, together with the shells and skeletons of billions of dead sea creatures. But beneath all the mud there is hard rock.

# The salty sea

A sailor who has spent much of his life at sea is often called an "old salt." This is a sort of joke, meaning that the sailor has probably been doused with so much sea water that he has become salty! For sea water is salty—so salty you can't drink it.

Why *is* the sea salty? Why isn't sea water fresh, like the water of rivers and lakes?

Many of the world's rivers start high in the mountains and flow down into the sea. As river water moves along, it dissolves billions of tiny bits of material out of the ground. Much of this material is salt. A river carries this dissolved salt with it until it reaches the sea. Thus, rivers dump tons of salt into the sea every day.

Scientists think the sea also gets some salt from inside the earth. They think that sea water flows through cracks in the sea bottom and comes back up through other cracks. As it flows beneath the bottom of the sea, it picks up salt from the rocks in the earth.

The sea has been collecting salt for thousands of millions of years. All this salt is spread through the sea by waves, winds, and currents. In fact, there is so much salt in the sea that if you spread it on the land it would cover all the land in the world with a layer of salt 150 feet (45 meters) high! This is why sea water tastes salty.

But if rivers have salt in them, why aren't *they* salty? And some rivers pour into lakes, so why aren't the lakes salty?

Well, rivers aren't salty because there's never very much salt in any one part of a river. Lakes that have rivers running into them aren't old enough to have collected much salt. Lakes are only thousands of years old, but the salty sea is thousands of millions of years old.

Many other chemicals are also in seawater. These chemicals got there the same way the salt did, but there is still more salt in the oceans than any other chemical. Scientists think the other chemicals get used up by sea creatures that take certain chemicals out of the water to make their shells and skeletons. Millions of trillions of creatures have done this for hundreds of millions of years.

Scientists think the sea is in balance now and that it has had about the same amount of salt for at least five hundred million years.

Salt from the sea has the shape of cubes. The salt you put on food is also tiny, tiny cubes.

In hot, dry countries, seawater is sometimes trapped in shallow pools. After the water dries up, salt is left behind.

# The colors of the sea

A glass of water has no color. But the water of the sea looks blue in some places and green in others. And in some places it looks brownish, or reddish, or even yellow. Where does the sea get its color?

The sea gets its blue color from sunlight. Sunlight is a mixture of all colors—red, blue, yellow, and so on. When sunlight falls upon the huge, deep mass of water in the sea, most of the colors are absorbed, or "soaked up." But the color blue is absorbed least of all. Most of the blue light is scattered through the water. So, the sea looks blue.

Where the sea looks green, it is usually because the water is filled with bits of clay

The sea's usual color is blue, but seawater can be any one of a number of colors. This picture shows red water meeting an area of blue-green water. The red color is caused by billions of tiny creatures in the water.

and other material. This has a yellowish-brown color, and when that color is mixed with the blue of the water, it makes the water green—just as when you mix blue and yellow paint together. And sometimes seawater is green because it is filled with great masses of tiny, greenish-yellow plants.

A reddish color is caused by a very thick, sort of "soupy" mix of tiny plants and animals and chemicals. It is usually found only near coasts. A yellowish color, such as that of the famous Yellow Sea off the coast of China, is caused by tons of tiny bits of yellowish dirt dumped into the sea by rivers.

Clouds passing across the sun can change the color of the sea. And so can the slant of the sun's rays as the sun moves across the sky.

# Wind over the water

If you've ever read a poem or story about the sea, you're sure to have read about waves. If you've ever been to a seashore, you've seen waves come rolling in to slap the sand with a splash. If you've been on the sea, you've not only seen waves, you've gone up and down on them. But what causes waves?

Fill a large bowl with water. Put your mouth close to the edge of the bowl and blow gently across the surface of the water. You'll see many small waves go skimming over the surface of the water. The wind of your breath caused the waves. Wind, passing over the water, is one of the main reasons for waves on the sea.

Waves are also caused by underwater earthquakes and by the pull of gravity of the moon and sun.

If you stand on the seashore on a windy day, watching the waves come rolling toward you, you will get the feeling that the whole sea is moving forward. But it isn't, really. As the wind passes over the water, it simply makes the top of the water sort of bob up and down. But the water doesn't move forward.

You can get an idea of how waves move by holding one end of a rope while a friend holds the other end. Now jiggle your end of the rope. You will see wave shapes pass along the rope toward your friend. But the rope isn't actually *moving* toward your friend. It can't move forward, because you're holding it. Only the *wave shapes* are moving.

When an ocean wave nears the shore, the water at the lower part of the wave begins to drag against the shallow bottom. As the wave slows down, the water in back of it begins to pile up, making the wave higher. When the water is shallow enough, the top of the wave spills over as a breaker.

The top of a wave is called the crest. The curved distance between two crests is called the trough (trawf).

Two children jiggle a rope to make a wave in it. The wave shape moves along the rope, but the rope stays in place. A wave in water works the same way. The shape moves forward, but the water only moves up and down.

41

When the tide is in, a beach may be covered with water. When the tide goes out, tiny pools of water, often with a few sea creatures in them, are left among the rocks.

# Tide in, tide out

"Get all the cargo aboard. We'll sail with the tide."

You've probably heard sea captains say this in movies or on television. But what do they mean? What *is* the tide? What are the high and low tides that sailors speak of?

If you visit a place by the sea, you'll find that the water creeps slowly up onto the land, then sinks slowly back again. This usually happens twice a day. This regular, daily movement of the sea is what we call tide.

In early morning, an ocean beach may be dry, silvery-gray sand. You can have a picnic on it, and build sand castles. But, about six hours later, the whole beach will be covered with water. The sea has *risen*, and we say the tide is "high" or "in." Then, about six hours after that, the beach can be seen again. It will be wet, and littered with driftwood and other things left behind as the water went back down. Now the tide is "low," or "out."

This rise and fall of the sea is caused by the turning of the earth and the tug of gravity from the moon and sun.

The moon's gravity tugs at the earth. It can't make the earth move much, because the earth is too big and heavy. But it does make the water move a bit. As the earth turns, the pull of the moon's gravity is strongest on the part of the earth that's facing the moon. The pull causes the sea at that place to bulge upward, making a high tide. Then, as that part of earth turns away from the moon, the sea sinks back down. It is low tide.

When the tide is high on one side of the earth, it is also high on the exact opposite side. Suppose it is six o'clock in the morning. The part of the sea you are looking at faces the moon and the tide is high. The earth turns completely around once every twenty-four hours. This means that, twelve hours later, at six o'clock at night, the earth will have turned halfway around. The part of the sea that you are looking at is now on the side of the earth farthest from the moon. And the tide will again be high.

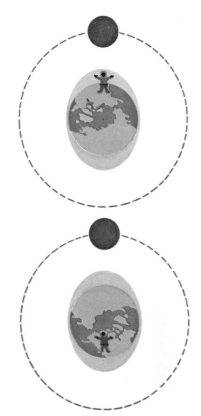

Ocean tides are caused mainly by the pull of the moon's gravity. High tide occurs directly below the moon and, at the same time, on the opposite side of the earth. The earth turns halfway around every twelve hours. So, there is a high tide at the same place every twelve hours.

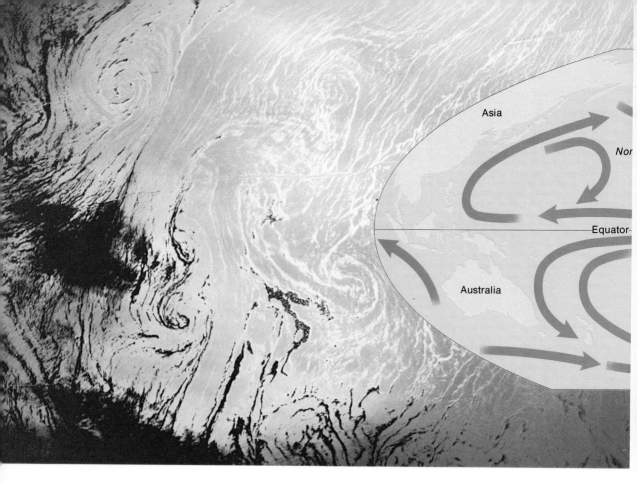

Swirling currents in the Ionian Sea can be seen in this photograph taken from a space shuttle. The thin lines crossing the currents are the wakes of ships.

Asia

Nor

Equator

Australia

# Rivers in the sea

Strange as it may seem, there are *rivers* in the sea—great, moving streams of water that are mightier than any river that runs through the land. These rivers are called *currents*, a word that means "running."

There are a great many currents, such as the Equatorial Current, the Gulf Stream, and the California Current. All of these currents run near the sea's surface and are easily seen. But there are also other currents that flow far below the surface of the sea.

The surface currents are important to people. For one thing, they affect the climate, making some places cold and others warm. For another thing, they affect the speed of ships. Hundreds of years ago, sailors found that sailing *with* a

The arrows show how ocean currents flow. North of the equator, currents flow clockwise. South of the equator, they flow counterclockwise.

current increases a ship's speed, while sailing *against* a current slows down a ship.

The surface currents are also important to the animal life in the sea. Many kinds of sea creatures drift with a current, letting it take them where it goes. These creatures are eaten by other sea animals. Thus, the surface currents that flow through the ocean bring food to many of the sea's dwellers.

Currents move mainly because of wind. But they are also helped by the heat of the sun and the rotation, or spin, of the earth.

Ocean currents start at the equator, earth's middle. There, strong winds, called the trade winds, push surface water westward. When a current reaches a continent, it is turned toward the north or the south.

The currents north of the equator flow in a clockwise direction. Those south of the equator flow counterclockwise. The currents form great, circular rivers, often with little "branches" curling away from them.

45

# People and the sea

# The first sea voyagers

For prehistoric people, the sea was a place where plenty of food could be found. They could wade in shallow water along the shore to gather clams and other shellfish. But they must certainly have wondered about the vast, mysterious place where this food came from. What other kinds of creatures lived in it? Did the water go on forever, or were there other lands beyond it? What was beneath it?

Finally, someone ventured out on the sea. People had probably seen floating logs, so the first "boat" may well have been several logs tied together with vines or strips of leather. Or, perhaps it was a large log, hollowed out so that one or two people could sit in it. But it was the first of all the ships that would sail the seas in the thousands of years to come.

People probably first used rafts and boats just to go a little way from shore in order to catch fish. But there must have come a day when two or three fishermen ventured out of sight of shore, or were blown out to sea by a storm. Perhaps they saw a distant island and paddled toward it. They would have been excited, and a bit afraid, because this was a new land. They had become explorers, using the sea as a road to a new place.

Long ago, people probably found new places by accident. Later, if these places were good places to live, people moved there on purpose. The sea became a way for people to spread out across the world.

The first sea voyage we know of took place more than thirty thousand years ago. People from somewhere in Southeast Asia crossed many miles of ocean to Australia, where no one then lived. We don't know whether these voyagers went to Australia on purpose. We don't know how they traveled, but they probably used rafts. We also don't know how long the voyage took. We do know that these people were the ancestors of the Aborigines, or native people, that European explorers met in Australia thousands of years later.

# Sea traders

Eight thousand years ago, a small, crude ship headed toward a little village on the coast of the land we now call Greece. The men on the ship were in high spirits. They had something very valuable, something that would make them all wealthy!

The little ship carried a load of shiny black stone—a stone we call obsidian (ahb SIHD ee uhn). Obsidian was wanted by people throughout Greece. At that time, all tools and weapons were made of stone. And obsidian was the best stone people could get. It was easily chipped to make sharp knives, axes, and spearpoints.

But obsidian was hard to get. It came from the island of Melos, far to the south. A voyage to Melos was very dangerous. This made the obsidian very valuable.

In those days, there was no such thing as money. People traded for the things they wanted. A chunk of obsidian might be worth a basket of wheat or several fine animal skins. The sailors who had obsidian to trade could become wealthy.

Those sailors of eight thousand years ago are the first sea traders we know of. Ever since, trading ships, called merchant ships, have sailed the seas, carrying goods from one land to another. The buying and selling that is done is still known as "trade."

The most famous traders of ancient times were the merchants of Phoenicia (fuh NIH shuh). Phoenicia lay along what is now the coasts of Syria, Israel, and Lebanon. And the merchant ships of Phoenicia traveled all over the Mediterranean Sea.

The Phoenicians traded purple cloth, glass, wine, and cedarwood for things that were of use to them. And because they braved the dangers of the sea, their cities became wealthy and famous.

All of these items were traded by ancient merchants who sailed the Mediterranean Sea.

# War on the water

A long line of ships lay rocking gently on the waves. The ships were really little more than big rowboats, about 120 feet (36 meters) long and twenty feet (6 m) wide. On each side there were three rows of oars, one row above the other. They were the kind of ships we call triremes (TRY reemz), meaning "three oars."

The rowers—170 of them—sat nervously gripping the wooden shafts of their oars. Small groups of men in bronze and leather armor, armed with spears or bows, stood about on the deck.

These were ships of war! The Greek navy was awaiting the coming of the enemy!

The time was about 2,500 years ago. The Mediterranean Sea was now a "highway" upon which many ships traveled. No land was safe against an invasion from the sea. And so, navies had been born—fleets of ships whose purpose was to fight off invaders or to carry soldiers from one place to another.

Little Greece had been invaded by the vast forces of the Persian Empire. The Persian army had already captured and burned Athens, the main city of Greece. And the great Persian fleet was now at anchor nearby.

The Greek leader, Themistocles (thuh MIHS tuh kleez), knew that the Persian fleet had to be defeated. The Persian army would then be without supplies or reinforcements. But how could he get the Persian ships to fight the smaller Greek fleet in a place where the Greeks might have an advantage?

Themistocles decided to trick the enemy. Pretending that he was a traitor, he sent a message to the Persian emperor, Xerxes (ZUHRK seez). The message said that the Greek fleet could be found off the island of Salamis (SAL uh muhs), about ten miles from Athens. But the ships were getting ready to sail. If Xerxes acted quickly, he could trap the Greeks and capture their entire navy.

The trick worked! Xerxes could not resist the chance to capture the Greek fleet. He ordered his ships to sail to Salamis.

Themistocles had chosen the place of battle well. To attack the Greeks, the Persian ships would have to pass through a narrow place, or channel. There was no way for the whole Persian fleet to attack at the same time. The huge Persian fleet—nearly a thousand ships— was in perfect formation. But as the ships entered the narrow channel, they had to bunch up, close together. The fleet quickly became a big, jumbled cluster.

The Greek fleet—less than four hundred ships—went into action. Rowing hard, the Greeks sped toward their foes. Some of the Greek ships passed the enemy, then turned. They began to push the Persian ships at the edge of the cluster back in toward the middle. Now the Persians were jammed even more tightly together.

By two's and three's, the Greek ships began to attack the Persian ships at the front of the cluster. The Persian ships at the rear could not help. Most of them couldn't move.

The Greeks rowed close to the enemy ships, breaking the Persians' oars on one side. Then the Greeks turned and rammed the helpless Persian ships in order to sink them. In other cases, Greek warriors stormed aboard many Persian ships and captured them.

The battle lasted for eight hours. Finally, the Persians at the rear, who hadn't even been able to get into the fight, turned and rowed their ships away. They could see that they were beaten. About two hundred Persian ships had been sunk and many others captured. The Greeks had lost only forty ships.

With so many ships gone, the Persian navy was no longer strong enough to keep the army supplied and reinforced. The following year, the Greek army defeated the Persian army and Greece was saved.

The Battle of Salamis, as it is called, gave the Greeks control of the sea. And, as the Greek leader Themistocles said, "Who controls the sea, controls everything!"

This is a copy of the kind of ship in which the Polynesians
sailed the Pacific Ocean more than two thousand years ago.

# Sailors of the South Sea

Most of the sailors who first explored the Mediterranean Sea were looking for new places to trade. But, long ago, other sailors set out to explore the Pacific Ocean in search of new places to live.

These people started out from somewhere in Southeast Asia. More than three thousand years ago they reached the islands of Tonga and Samoa. By about two thousand years ago, they were spreading out to find new homes on all the islands of the Pacific. They discovered Hawaii, to the north, New Zealand, to the south, and many other places. They were the people we now call Polynesians (pahl uh NEE shuhnz).

A Polynesian ship was two long canoes joined together side by side, with a space between. A deck was built over the space, and a small hut was built on the deck. These double canoes were moved by means of paddles, but they also had triangular sails made of woven plant leaves. Such a ship could carry as many as fifty people, together with pigs and other animals. The people also took young fruit and vegetable plants, to plant when they reached their new home.

The voyages that the Polynesians made in their small, rather frail ships were really quite wonderful. These people sailed across thousands of miles of open ocean, with only the sun, stars, wind, and waves to guide them. They were some of the world's truly great sailors!

# The dragon-ship sailors

*Seaward bound on a joyous journey.*
*Over breaking billows, with bellying sail*
*And a foamy beak, like a flying bird*
*The ship sped on. . . .*

These lines are from a poem written more than twelve hundred years ago. They tell of the beginning of a Viking voyage.

The Vikings were daring, skillful seamen from what are now the countries of Norway, Sweden, and Denmark. Indeed, *Viking* means "one who goes adventuring on the sea."

From about twelve hundred to nine hundred years ago, the Vikings roamed the Atlantic and the Mediterranean. The ships they sailed were sleek and fast. The front of a Viking ship was often carved into the shape of a fierce dragon head. For this reason, the ships became known as dragon ships.

A dragon ship was about eighty feet (24 meters) long and sixteen feet (5 m) wide. It could carry nearly a hundred men. About fifteen men sat on each side, pulling at the long oars that drove the ship through the water. A dragon ship also had a tall mast and a big sail that was hoisted when the wind was right.

These ships really weren't much more than long, light rowboats. But the Vikings sailed them across the unknown waters of the Atlantic Ocean. They discovered Iceland and Greenland. They even reached the shores of North America hundreds of years before Columbus was born.

# The age of exploration

About five hundred years ago, sailors from different parts of Europe began to make voyages of exploration. At first, they made short trips south, along the coast of Africa. But they were afraid to go very far. Many sailors believed that there were huge, horrible monsters in these unknown waters. And they thought that the sea far to the south was so hot it boiled!

The first Europeans to make these voyages were from the country of Portugal. They were sent forth by a Portuguese prince, known as Henry the Navigator. Henry was not a sailor, but he dreamed of making Portugal a great power. He intended to do this by sending expeditions to find new lands and treasures. His dream came true!

Sailors on Henry's ships discovered new islands in the Atlantic. They also landed at many places on the coast of Africa. They brought back gold and other valuable things.

Henry died in 1460, but Portuguese ships continued to explore southward into the Atlantic. Each successful voyage gave the sailors the courage to go farther the next time. In 1484, a Portuguese ship reached the equator before turning back. Then, in 1488, three Portuguese ships under the command of Bartolomeu Dias became the first to go around the southern tip of Africa. Dias named it the Cape of Good Hope, because it gave them hope of sailing around Africa to India. Just ten years later, in 1498, another Portuguese sailor, Vasco da Gama, did sail around Africa and all the way to India.

early globe, made about 1525

a Portuguese ship of Magellan's time

In the meantime, other European countries were also sending out men and ships to explore the world. One of these men was an Italian from Genoa, Italy, Christopher Columbus. Columbus sailed for the king and queen of Spain. He hoped to reach the Indies—by which he meant India, China, the East Indies and Japan—by sailing west across the Atlantic. Instead, he found a new world—America—in 1492.

John Cabot, also from Genoa, Italy, sailed in the service of England. He, too, hoped to reach the Indies by sailing west. Instead, he landed in North America in 1497.

Another man who thought he could find a western passage to India was Ferdinand Magellan. Although he was Portuguese, he found no support for his plan in Portugal. The Portuguese were content with the route around Africa. But Magellan did convince the king of Spain that his plan was a good one. The only reason no one had reached India by sailing west, Magellan said, was that they had not gone far enough south.

On September 20, 1519, Magellan left Spain with a fleet of five ships and about 240 men. Thirteen months later, they rounded South America through the stormy passage now called the Strait of Magellan. The new ocean they entered seemed very calm compared to the Atlantic. And so, Magellan named it the Pacific, or peaceful, Ocean.

By now the fleet was down to three ships. One had been wrecked and another had secretly sailed back to Spain. But Magellan pressed on. They reached the Philippines in March 1521. Here, Magellan was killed while helping in a war between two groups of Filipinos.

Finally, on September 6, 1522, one ship, the *Victoria*, commanded by Juan Sebastián del Cano, reached Spain with only eighteen men. They had been gone almost three years. They had not set out to do so, but they were the first to sail around the world.

These are a few of the many instruments sailors have used through the years to find their way while at sea. One of the astrolabes is more than seven hundred years old.

lodestone

pocket globe

astrolabes

# How did they find their way?

Pretend you're a sailor on a ship in the Mediterranean Sea, more than two thousand years ago. Your ship is out of sight of land. All around you, as far as you can see in any direction, there is only endless water.

Your ship does not have any of the special instruments that ships of today have. You have no charts, or maps, of the sea. So, how do you know that your ship is going where you want it to go? There is nothing on the water that you can sail toward—it all looks the same. How can you be sure your ship isn't going around in a big circle?

Finding your way about on the trackless ocean is called navigation. This word comes from two Latin words, *navis* meaning "ship" and *agere* meaning "to direct."

Sailors of long ago had ways of directing their ship to where they wanted to go. To go west, they kept their ship pointed

universal ring dial

quadrant

spyglass

compass

nocturnal

log glass

chronometer

toward where the sun sets—for the sun always sets in the west. They knew that if they kept the sun behind them in the morning, to their left during most of the day, and ahead of them in the late afternoon, they would always be heading west.

At night they used stars to keep on course. Sailors learned which part of the sky certain stars appeared in at different times of the year. And they knew that one star, the North Star, was always in the north.

Sailors could often tell where land was by means of clouds. Clouds usually pile up over land. When sailors saw a great pile of clouds in the distance, it usually meant there was land beneath the clouds.

As time went on, people invented instruments to take the guesswork out of navigation. But even with these instruments, many sailors still depend on "a star to steer her by."

# The sea battle that saved England

Great, black, iron anchors came sliding up out of the water. Huge sails began to billow as the wind pushed into them. Yellow and red banners snapped in the breeze. There were shouted orders, bugle calls, the creak of wooden boards, and the crackle of canvas sails in the wind. The ships of the Invincible Armada of Spain moved proudly out to sea.

It was the year 1588. The king of Spain had brought together a great fleet of 130 ships. This was Spain's Invincible Armada (which

This drawing, made in 1590, pictures the first attack against the Spanish Armada. Leaving Plymouth (upper right), the English ships sailed in two groups. One group went south and the other zig-zagged west (dotted lines), to get behind the huge Armada.

means "unbeatable armed force"). The Spanish were about to invade England!

The main ships of the Armada were twenty big warships called galleons. These great ships had high sides, a towering stern that rose high above the water, and rows of cannons on each side. In addition, there were forty-four large merchant ships that had been turned into warships, and a number of smaller ships that carried supplies or soldiers.

The English knew the Armada was coming, and they were ready. They, too, had galleons, but theirs were slimmer, lower, and faster than the Spanish galleons. They could move and turn more quickly. And, as it turned out, the English were better seamen.

As the Armada neared England, the English sailed out to attack. The English knew that the Spanish galleons would try to get as close as possible, so as to use their heavy, short-range cannon. At the same time, the Spanish soldiers crowded on the decks would open fire with their muskets. Then the Spaniards would hurl hooks, attached to ropes, to catch hold of the enemy ship and pull it close. Hundreds of Spanish soldiers would leap aboard, cut down the crew, and capture the ship.

Knowing this, the English adopted a simple plan. Their ships had light, long-range cannon that could fire a cannonball much farther than the heavier Spanish guns. And, with their faster ships, they knew they could outsail the Spanish galleons. So, they would sail back and forth out of range of the Spanish guns as they bombarded the enemy.

Off and on, over the next six days, this is

the way the battle went. The Armada continued to make its way up the English Channel, the strip of sea that separates England from France. Some Spanish ships were sunk or captured. No English ships were lost. But neither side could win a victory. The Spanish, however, were running out of cannonballs. The English, on the other hand, simply sailed into nearby English ports, got more cannonballs, and rejoined the fight.

On the evening of the seventh day, the Spanish ships anchored at the port of Calais, on the coast of France, across from England. The English could not come into the harbor after them. This would have brought them too close to the Spanish ships. But the English captains had a plan ready. They knew how to make the Spaniards come out of the harbor.

Shortly before dawn, Spaniards on watch saw eight ships moving toward them. Suddenly, the ships burst into flames! The English had steered the ships into the harbor and then set them afire. If these fire ships got among the anchored Spanish vessels, dozens would be set ablaze. In panic, the Spanish captains cut the ropes that held their anchors and hoisted sail. In the dark, and in their haste to get out of the harbor, many of the Spanish ships crashed into each other.

This was exactly what the English had hoped for! Now the Armada was simply a great jumble of ships. As the sun began to rise, the English attacked!

All day long they dashed in and out among the Spaniards, pounding them with cannonballs. But as night came on, a sudden

storm broke. The ships on both sides had to
stop fighting and look to their safety in the
howling wind and driving rain. The battle
came to an end.

Driven north by the storm, the Armada had
to sail all the way around the British Isles.
Most of the ships were badly damaged and
leaking. Many sank. Others, driven helplessly
before the wind, were wrecked on the rocky
shore of Ireland. Thousands of men lost their
lives. Of the 130 ships that sailed, only 67 got
home again.

# Pirates!

Throughout history there have been sea-going robbers called pirates. The word *pirate* comes from an ancient Greek word that means "to attack." Pirates got their name because they attacked helpless ships and seacoast towns. There was nothing brave or glamorous about pirates. They were criminals.

About 450 to 250 years ago, hundreds of pirate ships sailed under the "Jolly Roger," a black flag with a white skull and crossed bones on it. Manned by bloodthirsty crews they roamed the seas in search of riches.

Pirates usually hunted for unarmed merchant ships. When one was sighted, the pirate ship would chase it down, often crippling it with cannon fire. Then the pirates would swarm aboard, killing anyone who resisted them and seizing everything of value they could find.

But, as time went on, it became harder and harder for pirates to continue their bloody trade. Some were hunted down and killed. Others were pardoned if they promised to give up piracy. But the stories of these fierce and bloodthirsty sea bandits are still a part of the lore of the sea.

One pirate almost everyone has heard of was Captain William Kidd. Yet Kidd started out as an honest man, the captain of a merchant ship. Then, about 1695, some powerful men in England talked Kidd into becoming a hunter of pirates. These men, and Kidd, hoped to rid the seas of pirates—and take for themselves all the treasure the pirates had stolen.

Kidd sailed for months, but never caught a single pirate. Finally, growing desperate, he decided to become a pirate himself. He and his men began to attack merchant ships in the Indian Ocean, off the east coast of Africa. They soon had an enormous treasure.

Because he had not attacked any English ships, Kidd must have thought that he would not be accused of piracy. In 1699 he sailed to the West Indies with all his treasure. But there he learned that the English government had declared him a pirate.

One of the men who had talked him into hunting for pirates was now the governor of Boston. Kidd, thinking he might use his treasure to bargain for his life and obtain a pardon, immediately sailed for Boston.

But it was no use. The governor had Captain Kidd arrested and sent to England. And there, in 1701, Kidd was hanged for the crime of piracy. To this day, no one knows what happened to most of his treasure.

Another pirate, known as "Blackbeard," was a fierce and bloodthirsty man who struck fear into the heart of all who knew him.

This man's real name was Edward Teach. He got his nickname from the thick tangle of coal-black beard that covered most of his face. In battle, he looked like a devil. He twisted his beard into pigtails that he tied with ribbons. And he stuck long, slow-burning matches into his hat.

Early in the 1700's, Blackbeard, in his ship *Queen Anne's Revenge,* was the terror of the Caribbean Sea. He plundered any ship unlucky enough to cross his path, and quickly gathered a huge fortune. After a time, he sailed north and began to attack shipping along the coast of Virginia and North Carolina.

Finally, the leaders of these British colonies secretly outfitted two small ships to go after Blackbeard. The ships were placed under the command of a courageous officer, Lieutenant Robert Maynard.

Maynard discovered that Blackbeard kept his ship in hiding in a certain small inlet. On a morning in 1718, Maynard led his two small ships into the bay. Blackbeard opened fire with his cannons. But Maynard's ship reached the pirate vessel and he and his men leaped aboard the other ship. In the fierce fight that followed, Blackbeard was shot in the stomach and cut on the neck by a cutlass. But he continued to fight until he fell dead, probably from loss of blood. Eight other pirates were killed, and the rest surrendered.

Most pirates were killed or hanged for their crimes. But one famous pirate was made a knight and a governor by the King of England!

This pirate's name was Henry Morgan. When he was a young man England and Spain were at war. Morgan soon gained a reputation as a brave and clever fighting man. In 1668, he was put in command of a number of ships and men. With this force he began to attack Spanish towns in Cuba and Panama. He was extremely successful, and captured a lot of treasure.

Morgan was indeed a clever, skillful commander. In 1671 he attacked Panama City in Panama. But instead of attacking from the sea, Morgan marched his men across the land and captured the city from the rear. After taking a huge treasure, he burned the city to the ground.

But Morgan's raid was made after a treaty of peace had been signed between England and Spain—and Morgan knew this. The Spanish king demanded that he be punished for piracy.

Henry Morgan was arrested and taken to England. But Morgan was a hero to the English people, who hated Spain. So instead of hanging Morgan, the king made him a knight and appointed him assistant governor of the island of Jamaica. Morgan became a respectable man. Unlike most pirates, he died peacefully in bed.

Two famous pirates were women. They were Anne Bonney and Mary Read. In the early 1700's they were part of the crew of a ship commanded by a pirate known as Calico Jack Rackham.

These two women were ferocious and skillful fighters, and had the respect of all the men in the crew. In fact, Mary Read once fought a duel for a young man with whom she had fallen in love. Although the pirate she fought was a big, burly man, and a tough fighter, Mary killed him and walked away unharmed.

Calico Jack's ship was finally captured. Mary and Anne were put on trial with the rest of the crew. All the men were hanged. Mary Read died in prison, of fever. But Anne Bonney was spared, for she was about to have a baby. No one knows what became of her.

Mary Read was a pirate of the 1700's. She was a fierce and skillful fighter.

# The whalers

"Thar she blows!"

That was the cry that sent the men of an old-time whaling ship into action—the cry that meant a whale had been sighted. Quickly, boats were lowered onto the sea. Each boat had a crew of men to row, and a harpooner. It was the harpooner's job to drive his long spear into the whale's body. Pulling hard at the oars, the boat crews hurled their crafts through the water toward the whale. Hunting these giant creatures was their work.

But it was dangerous work, for boats could be smashed and men injured and drowned. When the boat was near enough, the harpooner hurled his big spear. Then began what American whalers from Nantucket called "The Nantucket sleigh ride." The harpoon was attached to the boat by a long rope. As the wounded whale swam to get away, it towed the boat through the water at tremendous speed.

In time, the whale tired and slowed. The whalers then killed the great creature with spearlike weapons. Its body was towed back to the ship and cut up. The fat was boiled down into oil and stored in barrels.

Whales have been hunted for thousands of years. Prehistoric people hunted them for their rich, red meat. Later, whales were hunted for their fat and bone as well. About 150 years ago, whale oil was widely used for lamps and for making candles. This was the time when hundreds of ships hunted whales

in all the seas of the world. The whaling
crews were often away for four or five years
at a time.

Today, most countries protect whales.
There is a limit to the number that can be
killed. Even so, many kinds of these big,
marvelous animals may soon be extinct.

(above) The picture shows
a whale hunt from long
ago. (right) The harpooner
threw a harpoon, or long
spear.

The clipper ship *David Crockett* was built at Mystic, Connecticut, in 1853. She was one of many famous clippers, the fastest sailing ships ever built. The *David Crockett* rounded Cape Horn forty-eight times—more times than any other sailing ship in history.

# The last great days of sail

The clipper ships were among the most beautiful—and the fastest—sailing ships ever built. They were long, low, and slim. Their towering masts carried great clouds of billowing sails. They were called "clippers" because it was said they "clipped off" miles as swiftly as a barber clips off hair.

One of the first clipper ships was the *Rainbow*. It was launched in New York in 1845. Many seamen felt that the *Rainbow* was too slim and light to stand the pounding of a stormy sea. They said she would turn over from the weight of all her spars—the masts and wooden crosspieces that held the sails. But none of these things happened. The *Rainbow* proved to be so fast that other shipbuilders were soon making ships just like her.

Clipper ships quickly began to set new speed records. They made voyages from New England to China and Australia in half the time it took other ships. In 1854, the clipper ship *Champion of the Seas* sailed 465 miles (748 kilometers) in twenty-four hours. That was the fastest that any ship had ever sailed. Not until twenty-five years later did a steamship go faster.

Clipper ships carried cargo, and sometimes passengers, to and from most parts of the world. For a time they were "queens" of the sea. But their time was short. By the 1860's they were being replaced by bulkier ships that were slower, but could carry more cargo and needed fewer sailors. And in the 1860's and 1870's, steamships began to take the place of sailing ships. The clippers were among the last of the great sailing ships.

# The "unsinkable" ship

On a bright, clear, and cold night in April, 1912, a sleek, giant ship plowed through the waters of the North Atlantic. The ship was moving at a speed of about twenty-two knots (25 miles or 41 kilometers) an hour. This was too fast, for there had been many warnings by radio that the water ahead was dotted with icebergs.

The ship was named *Titanic*, a word that means "huge." It was well-named, for it was the largest ship in the world—882.5 feet (269 meters) long. It was the kind of ship known as a luxury liner, a kind of floating hotel. It contained hundreds of beautiful rooms for passengers, as well as game rooms, dining rooms, and a gymnasium.

The *Titanic* was a brand-new ship. In fact, this was her first voyage. People said she was unsinkable. The builders had divided the lower part of the ship into sixteen watertight compartments. Even if as many as four of these should fill with water, the air in the others would keep the ship afloat. "God Himself could not sink this ship," a member of the crew had boasted before the *Titanic* sailed.

The *Titanic* was sailing from Southampton, England, to New York City. All together, counting passengers and crew, there were more than two thousand people aboard. As the brightly lighted ship sped through the night,

This is the *Titanic* as it left England at the start of its first—and only—voyage.

The *Titanic* was a luxury liner. It had hundreds of beautiful passenger cabins like this one.

most of those on board were asleep in their cabins, confident of their safety.

A little before midnight, a sailor on lookout duty sighted a large iceberg in the ship's path. He picked up the phone to the bridge, the place from which the ship was steered.

"Iceberg! Right ahead!"

At once, the officer on duty ordered the steersman to make a sharp turn. For a moment, it seemed as if the ship must crash into the iceberg. Then, at the last instant, the ship veered away. It passed the towering, jagged mass of ice so closely that anyone standing on deck might have reached out and touched it.

But as the *Titanic* slid past the iceberg, there was a faint grinding noise. The ship seemed to shudder slightly.

Many passengers were awakened by the

noise and the jar. Others, still awake, heard the sound and felt the jar. Some went out on deck to see what had happened.

The *Titanic*'s captain, a white-bearded man named Edward Smith, rushed to the bridge from his cabin nearby. Quickly, he ordered men to check to see what damage had been done. They found that the iceberg, hard as rock and sharp as a knife, had sliced a gash three hundred feet (90 meters) long in the ship's bottom. Water was pouring into six compartments. The men looked at one another in shock. There was no doubt—the *Titanic* was going to sink!

The captain issued orders. The ship's radio operator was told to send out signals for help. Members of the crew hurried down the ship's corridors, waking passengers and helping them into life jackets. Most people were a bit anxious, but there was no panic. They were not told that the ship was going to sink— most of them wouldn't have believed it anyway.

The crew uncovered the lifeboats and made them ready. But there was a terrible problem. There were only enough boats for about half the people aboard.

According to the law of the sea, women and children were put into the lifeboats first. Husbands kissed their wives good-by, fathers kissed their children. Many women refused to get into the boats, not wishing to leave their husbands. Some men went, members of the crew and others who could row the boats. Many people were left aboard, but they still thought that everyone would be saved. Help was surely on the way. And besides, the *Titanic* couldn't *really* sink—could it?

As the lifeboats were lowered into the black, cold water, a ship was seen on the horizon, less than twenty miles (32 kilometers) away. Help was at hand! At once, signal rockets were fired. They streaked up into the sky to explode with a bang and a flash of white stars.

But there was no reply from the other ship. Nor was there any response to the distress signals sent out by radio. Months later, it was learned that this ship, the *Californian*, had stopped for the night because of the ice. Her radio operator, who had been on duty for more than fifteen hours, went to bed only twenty minutes before the *Titanic* hit the iceberg.

The lifeboats began to pull away from the *Titanic*. Everyone now knew that the ship was indeed sinking. Its bow, or front, was much lower in the water than the stern, or rear. Slowly, the stern rose into the air. Many of the people left on board jumped into the icy water, hoping to swim to a boat or find a piece of floating wreckage to which they could cling.

Minutes dragged by while the people in the boats stared, unbelieving, too shocked and stunned even to cry. The bow of the ship was now underwater. The stern was lifting ever higher. The water around the sinking ship was filled with floating objects—chairs, tables, shuffleboard sticks . . . and people swimming for their lives.

Slowly, the *Titanic*'s stern lifted until it was pointing straight up at the sky. Then, gently, it sloped back and the ship slid beneath the surface. With a last swirl, the water closed over the "unsinkable" ship.

A few—a very few—of those who had jumped overboard, or had been washed overboard as the ship went down, managed to reach a boat. Many people were trapped on the sinking ship. Others died in the icy water.

From the time it grazed the iceberg, the *Titanic* had taken just two hours and forty minutes to sink. Now, for more than another hour and a half, the people in the boats fought to stay alive. It was bitter cold, and many were only half dressed. Most were soaked to the skin. A few died, of shock and cold.

Finally, at four o'clock in the morning, with the sun rising over a calm sea dotted with floating icebergs, the ship *Carpathia* arrived. She had steamed fifty-eight miles at top speed. Quickly, the frozen, stunned survivors were taken aboard. There were only 705 of them. Some 1,500 people had died in the disaster—victims of the sea.

# The battle of Midway

On a June day in 1942, Japanese warships steamed toward the tiny island of Midway in the Pacific Ocean. Japan and the United States were at war. Midway was an important American base. Whoever controlled it controlled a large part of the Pacific Ocean.

The Japanese intended to capture Midway in a surprise attack. They were sure that the American fleet would try to recapture the island. Then the Japanese, who had many more ships, would destroy the American fleet and win the war.

But the Americans had some surprises of their own. True, they were badly outnumbered. The Japanese had four aircraft carriers and more than forty other ships. The Americans had three carriers and twenty-two other ships. But this was two more carriers than the Japanese thought they had.

The biggest surprise of all was that the Americans had figured out the Japanese secret code! They knew how many ships the Japanese had and exactly where they were. So the Americans were ready to spring a surprise attack of their own.

Early on the morning of June 4, more than one hundred planes from Japanese aircraft carriers roared over Midway, dropping bombs. The battle had begun!

A short time later, planes from the American carriers took off to search for the Japanese ships. The first to find them were forty-one planes armed with torpedoes. Flying low over the water, straight at the Japanese carriers, they launched their torpedoes. All but six of the planes were shot down, without doing any damage.

But then, three squadrons of American dive bombers found the Japanese carriers. They came shrieking down from high in the sky. Their bombs hit three of the Japanese carriers, causing them to burst into flames.

But in the meantime, planes from the fourth Japanese carrier found one of the American carriers. They hit it with three bombs and two torpedoes. The carrier was so badly damaged its crew had to abandon it.

After going back to refuel and get more bombs for their planes, the Americans took off after the last Japanese carrier. When they found it, they hit it with four bombs. Like the American carrier, it was so badly damaged its crew had to leave it.

The Americans had lost one carrier and many planes. But the Japanese had lost all their carriers and all their planes. Without planes, they couldn't protect their other ships from the American dive bombers. The Japanese admiral ordered his ships to turn back to Japan. The battle was over, and Japan had lost.

The Americans had won control of the sea. And, in time, this would help them to win the war against Japan.

# Beneath the pole

Above the endless sheet of white ice, a cold wind howled. Somewhere in all that frozen whiteness was the spot that was the farthest north of any place on earth—the North Pole.

Beneath the ice lay the dark, chill waters of the Arctic Ocean. A long, slim, metal shape slid through the black water. It was a ship— the United States Navy nuclear-powered submarine *Nautilus* (NAW tuh luhs).

The *Nautilus* had been moving beneath the ice for nearly three full days. Now, the men of the crew waited eagerly for what was about to happen. The ship was silent except for the steady *ping . . . ping . . . ping* of the sonar. This sensitive instrument told the crew that the polar ice above the ship was from eight to eighty feet (2.4 to 24 meters) thick. The needle on the depth gauge showed that the ship was four hundred feet (122 m) below the surface.

Then the voice of the captain came over the ship's loudspeakers. "Stand by! Ten . . . eight . . . six . . . four . . . three . . . two . . . one. MARK! August 3, 1958. Time, 2315 (11:15 P.M.). For the United States and the United States Navy—the North Pole!"

There were cheers. For, at that moment, the *Nautilus* became the first ship to ever sail beneath the ice at the North Pole. The *Nautilus* had traveled from the Pacific Ocean to the Atlantic Ocean, across the top of the world.

Then, two years later, in 1960, another United States nuclear-powered submarine, the *Triton*, sailed around the world underwater. The voyage of the *Triton* covered 41,500 miles (66,790 kilometers) and lasted a total of eighty-four days.

The voyages of the *Nautilus* and the *Triton* were more than historic firsts. They proved the importance of submarines as a way to reach new places and learn new things.

# Queens of the sea

Today's queens of the sea are giant merchant ships that carry trade goods all over the world. Compared to these giants, the ships of the ancient Phoenician traders would look like tiny rowboats!

The Phoenician traders would be amazed if they could see how modern merchant ships are loaded. Big cranes and derricks swing out over the side of the ship to lift the cargo aboard. On some kinds of ships, hundreds of cars and trucks can be driven up a ramp and through large openings in the ship's side.

Many merchant ships of today are the kind called container ships. Cargo of all kinds is loaded into large, metal containers. These containers are then neatly stacked, side by side and on top of each other. The largest container ships are about seven hundred feet (210 meters) long. They can carry more than a thousand containers.

Cargoes of liquid, such as oil, are carried in huge ships called tankers. The largest of these, sometimes called supertankers, are about a quarter of a mile (four-tenths of a kilometer) long and almost as wide as a twenty-lane highway. The inside of a tanker is like a big ice cube tray, each square filled with oil.

Until recently, the "queens of the sea" were big passenger liners. These ships were like floating hotels that carried hundreds of people across the sea. Now, most people prefer to travel by airplane. But many passenger liners are still in use, making short cruises for people who enjoy a sea voyage.

The deck of this supertanker is longer than four football fields.

These fish were caught in the sea near Ghana. People living near the sea eat a lot of fish.

# Food from the sea

Today, more than ever, the sea is an important source of food.

Fish has always been an important food, especially for people who live on islands and along coasts. Thirty thousand years ago, people fished from the shore. They tied pointed slivers of bone to long lines made of woven grass or animal skin. The lines were dropped into the water. When a fish swallowed the bone, the bone stuck in its throat and the fish could be pulled in.

In time, people began to use boats when they went fishing. They also found a way to catch more fish at once—with nets. All over the world, for thousands of years, fishing boats have sailed out each morning, seeking a day's catch of fish. Even today, men in small boats sail out to catch fish by dropping lines or nets into the water.

But most large nations now have fleets of huge ships with electronic devices for finding fish and machinery for hauling them in. Millions of tons of fish are taken from the sea every year. This is valuable and important food that is badly needed.

Of course, fish is not the only food that comes from the sea. Crustaceans such as lobsters, crabs, and shrimp are also an important food. So are many mollusks—oysters, clams, scallops, and squid. People have hunted all of these creatures for thousands of years.

Lobsters are caught in traps. The traps are baited with a piece of fish and dropped into the water. When a lobster crawls into the trap it can't get out again. A lobster fisher pulls up his traps every day or so. Shrimp and crabs are caught in nets. Long ago, oysters were hunted by divers who swam down and plucked them up by hand. Today, large numbers of oysters are scooped up by machines called dredges.

Many of the creatures living in the sea have been—or still are—hunted by people. Since prehistoric times the sea has been a hunting ground because it is a rich source of food and other materials. It will continue to be a hunting ground for a long time.

A variety of fresh fish and other seafood is available at this fish market restaurant in Belgium.

# The challenge of the sea

The sea is a place of danger. For this very reason, it is also a challenge. People are willing to defy its dangers, to risk their lives, so as to conquer it in some way. And many of them have done it alone! In 1876, a fisherman named Alfred Johnson set out to become the first person to sail alone across the Atlantic. He started from Gloucester, Massachusetts, and reached Wales forty-six days later. His small boat, the *Centennial*, was only twenty feet (6 meters) long.

In 1896, two Americans decided to row across. George Firbo and Frank Samuelson took fifty-five days to row their boat from New York City to the Scilly Islands, just off the coast of England. Their boat was eighteen feet (5.4 m) long.

On April 24, 1895, an American, Joshua Slocum, set out to become the first person to sail alone around the world. His boat, the *Spray*, was only a little more than thirty-six feet (10.8 m) long. He made a lot of stops, and his trip took about three years.

In 1969, Robin Knox-Johnston of Great Britain became the first person to sail alone around the world without making any stops. His voyage took 313 days.

In that same year, John Fairfax of Great Britain became the first person to row alone across the Atlantic. It took him 180 days.

In 1978, Naomi James of New Zealand became the first woman to sail alone around the world by way of Cape Horn, at the tip of South America.

Those who challenge the sea do not always win. Many men and women have sailed off, never to be seen again. But if there were no danger, there would be no challenge.

Naomi James, who sailed alone around the world in 1978, uses a sextant to find out where she is.

# Exploring the depths

A slender, baldheaded man with a bushy moustache sat inside a hollow, metal ball. He peered excitedly through a round window. The man was Professor William Beebe. Next to him was Otis Barton, the man who had designed the metal ball. The two men were 2,200 feet (660 meters) beneath the surface of the sea—deeper than anyone had ever gone before.

The metal ball was a bit like a weight on the end of a fishing line. It hung from a thick metal cable attached to a ship, above. The ball, which was barely big enough for Beebe and Barton to sit in, had been given the name *bathysphere* (BATH uh sfihr), meaning "depth ball." Its metal walls were an inch and a half (4 centimeters) thick. Two tanks of oxygen provided enough air for eight hours.

The water was pitch-black, for light cannot penetrate so far down into the sea. But the ball was equipped with a searchlight that lit up the water for a short distance. And in the beam of light, Beebe could see many strange creatures that no one had ever seen before.

He saw two big fish whose bodies were outlined by rows of pale blue, glowing lights. There were small fish with orange lights on their heads, bluish-white bodies, and long fangs in their upper jaws.

It might seem easy to go deep down into the sea. But it's not. The deeper you go into the sea, the more water there is above you. Water has weight that presses against you. And the deeper you go, the greater the pressure. Even a thick-walled container made of sturdy metal

These pictures show six kinds of underwater diving craft—called submersibles—and the depths to which they go.

bathysphere
3,028 ft.
(923 m)

Deepstar 4000
4,000 ft.
(1,219 m)

*Deep Rover*
3,300 ft.
(1,000 m)

*Cyana*
9,843 ft.
(3,000 m)

*Alvin*
12,000 ft.
(3,658 m)

bathyscaph
*Trieste*
35,800 ft.
(10,910 m)

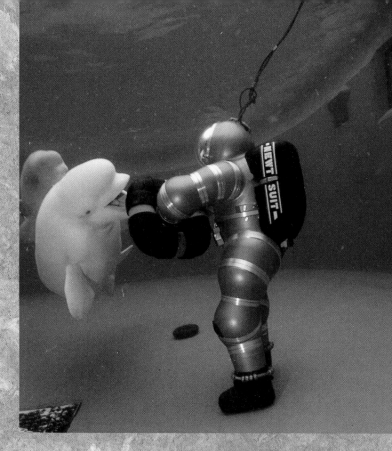

A diver in a Newtsuit can work underwater at depths up to 1,000 feet (300 meters). The suit is aluminum, and the joints turn instead of bending. This diver is testing the suit in an aquarium tank.

could, if it went too deep, be crushed by the weight of all the water pressing on it.

It took a lot of courage for the two men to let themselves be lowered to the depth they had reached. If the cable should break, they were doomed! The bathysphere would sink until the pressure of the water crushed it like an egg. But Barton, an engineer, was sure of the safety of his machine. And Beebe was a scientist, willing to risk his life for knowledge.

Beebe and Barton made their deepest dives in 1932. They were the first to brave such depths. We gained a great deal of knowledge of deep-sea life from the careful notes that Beebe made about the things he saw.

Since that time, other men, in other kinds of vessels, have gone far deeper. They have added to our knowledge of the undersea world.

A Swiss scientist, Auguste Piccard, invented

a deep-sea diving ship called a bathyscaph (BATH uh skaf), a name that means "deep ship." The bathyscaph does not have to be lowered on a cable as the bathysphere was. It can move up and down by itself.

In 1960, Piccard's son Jacques and Don Walsh, an American naval officer, took the bathyscaph *Trieste* down 35,800 feet (10,910 meters) into the Pacific Ocean. This dive of nearly seven miles (11 kilometers) is the deepest ever made.

Once a bathyscaph is down, it cannot move forward or backward very easily. But another kind of deep-sea ship, called a submersible, moves very well underwater. As yet, however, submersibles can go down only about twelve thousand feet (3,658 meters).

Some deep-sea exploring is done in specially built submersibles. In 1977, scientists in such a submersible explored parts of a great crack that lies two miles (3.2 kilometers) down on the rocky floor of the Pacific Ocean. This crack, or rift, is a place where melted rock from deep inside the earth oozes up onto the ocean floor.

Down in these cold, black depths, the explorers made an amazing discovery. Usually, there aren't many animals at such depths. But there were animals there—lots of them. Through cracks in the sea bottom, warm water spurted up. And in these patches of warm water, like islands in the cold, lived animals seldom seen so deep.

The deep sea is like a new world, almost as strange as another planet. And we are really only beginning to explore it. It is full of mysteries, new discoveries, and exciting things to learn!

# A place for fun

The sea has long been a place to have fun. Today, more people than ever before enjoy swimming, sailing, fishing, skin diving, surfing, water-skiing, and other water sports.

Children play on the beach in Puerto Rico.

Kite flying on the Oregon coast is fun.

Windsurfing is a popular sport.

Lobster is the main dish at this picnic.

Kenai Peninsula, Alaska

(above) Workers clean up after an oil spill. The oiled dirt is bagged and removed so that plants and animals can once again live off the land and water. (right) A bird rescue worker holds a common loon that died as a result of an oil spill.

# The sea in danger

For millions of years, the sea was clean and filled with life. But today, it is in danger.

Throughout the once-clean ocean there are now great floating patches of scum and tarry gobs of oil. Mixed into the water are many kinds of poisonous chemicals. Hundreds of places where sea creatures once lived are now empty of life. In many places where people have taken food from the sea for thousands of years, it is no longer safe to do so. Many sea creatures are so filled with poison that to eat them means sickness or death.

Why have these terrible things happened to the sea? There are many reasons.

Many factories use large amounts of water for cooling hot machines, for washing materials, and for mixing with chemicals. These factories were built where there is plenty of water, next to rivers or at the sea's edge. Tons of water are pumped into the factories every day. After the water is used, most of it is poured back into the sea, or into rivers that carry it to the sea. Often, this used water contains poisonous chemicals. And these chemicals are polluting the ocean.

The sea is also polluted by oil spilled by huge tankers, and by sewage that pours into the water from thousands of cities.

It took people a long time to realize that the sea is in danger. But now, scientists and many others are fighting to save the sea. Laws have been passed to prevent harmful things from being put into the water. It will be a long and hard job to save the sea. But it is a job that must be done.

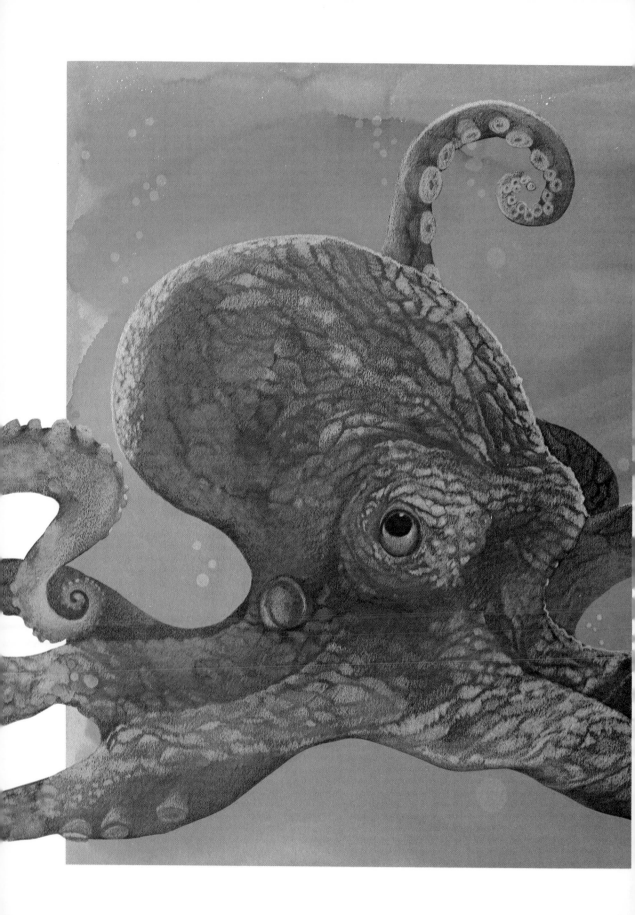

# Animals of the sea

# Life in the sea

The sea is filled with many different kinds of plants and animals. Some live in warm, tropical waters and others live in cold, polar seas. Some live close to shore and some live far from land. Some live close to the surface and some live deep down in the ocean.

The plants of the ocean, like those of the land, depend upon sunlight for their life. For sunlight contains energy, and all living things need this energy to stay alive. Sea plants, like most land plants, take the energy in sunlight and turn it into food. They store this food and use it a little at a time.

Some sea animals get their energy by eating plants. Other animals get their energy by eating the plant-eaters. And animals that live in the deepest, darkest parts of the ocean get their energy from plants and animals that live above them, die, and drift down. This way of passing energy along is called the food chain.

The food chain of the ocean begins with tiny plants such as those called diatoms (DY uh tahms). Diatoms drift on or near the

Billions of tiny plants and animals drift in huge groups in the sea. These creatures are so small that most of them can be seen only with a microscope.

surface. They are so tiny that you need a microscope to see them. But when billions of them drift together, they color the water green.

Diatoms look like no plant you have ever seen. They have no roots, leaves, or stems. A diatom is just a blob of greenish-brown jelly inside a two-piece, glassy shell.

There are many different kinds of these tiny plants. The shells of some are square, others are round, or shaped like pillows, rods, or stars. Some diatoms float alone; others join together in long chains.

Drifting and swimming within the huge clouds of diatoms are billions of other little living things. Some are tiny animals, no bigger than the plants. Some are the eggs of fish and other creatures. Some are newly hatched baby clams, worms, lobsters, snails, and other animals. Some are tiny, shrimplike animals called copepods (KOH puh pahdz).

These huge masses of drifting plants and animals are called plankton (PLANGK tuhn), a word that means "wandering." The plankton is like a great "meadow" where all kinds of animals live and eat. In fact, it is often called "the pasture of the sea."

The copepods and some of the other tiny animals in the plankton feed on the diatoms. And these animals, in turn, are eaten by small fish and other animals that stay in or near the plankton to be near their food. Large animals, such as tuna and dolphin, feed on the small fish. And even bigger animals, such as sharks, eat both big and little fish.

Thus, around, above, and below the plankton there are many kinds of swimming

animals. Most are fish, but there are also squid, whales, turtles, and other creatures.

Although these animals swim about, they can't live just anywhere. Some can live only in warm water; others only in cold water. Some, because of the way their bodies are made, can live only at certain depths. If they swim too far up or down, the change in the pressure of the water might kill them.

Both animals and plants live on the bottom. Animals are found in shallow water near shore and in the depths of the ocean. But plants cannot live any deeper than sunlight can reach. In clear water, sunlight reaches down only about six hundred feet (180 meters). Then the water grows darker and darker. Finally, below about seventeen hundred feet (510 m), the water is pitch-black.

Most kinds of the leafy plants that are usually called seaweed grow in shallow water near shore. Masses of seaweed form underwater forests in which many kinds of animals live. For some of these animals the seaweed is food. For others, it is a good hiding place. For still others, it is a rich hunting ground where they can find many animals to eat.

Many bottom-dwelling animals walk or crawl about. Some can swim and some cannot. Others, such as oysters, attach themselves to the bottom. They spend their entire adult life in one place. Some food drifts down to them. And some is carried to them by currents and tides.

When a sea animal dies, it slowly sinks. Its body is usually eaten by animals living at lower depths. And when these animals die, they sink down and become food for creatures that live even deeper, or that live on the bottom.

Dead animals that are not eaten sink to the bottom. Their bodies slowly break down into chemicals. These chemicals spread through the water and provide food for plants. And so the food chain starts all over again.

The sea, like the land, is a place where every creature depends upon other creatures for life—and all life depends upon the sun.

Tiny sea plants are eaten by little animals. These animals are eaten by small fish. Large fish and other animals eat smaller creatures. Dead animals and plants rot and put chemicals into the water. Tiny plants use the chemicals. Thus, all the plants and animals in the sea are part of a great food chain.

**Fish** Many people think of any animal that lives in the sea as a fish. But only a certain kind of animal with a certain kind of body is a fish. Such creatures as oysters, starfish, jellyfish, and whales *aren't* fish.

All fish have a backbone. Oysters, starfish, and jellyfish don't have a backbone or any skeleton at all. So, they aren't fish.

All fish are what we call cold-blooded. A fish's body temperature changes with the temperature of the water it's in. But a whale is warm-blooded. Its body temperature is always the same. Thus, a whale isn't a fish.

Most fish have thin folds of skin, called gills, on each side of the head. To breathe, a fish takes water into its mouth. As the water goes over the gills, oxygen is taken out of the water and passed into the fish's blood.

Most fish have fins and scaly skins. A fin is made up of thin strips of bone covered with thin skin. Fish use their fins to help them swim, to steer, and to keep their balance.

So, all fish have a backbone and all fish are cold-blooded. Most have gills, fins, and scales. These are the things that make a fish a fish.

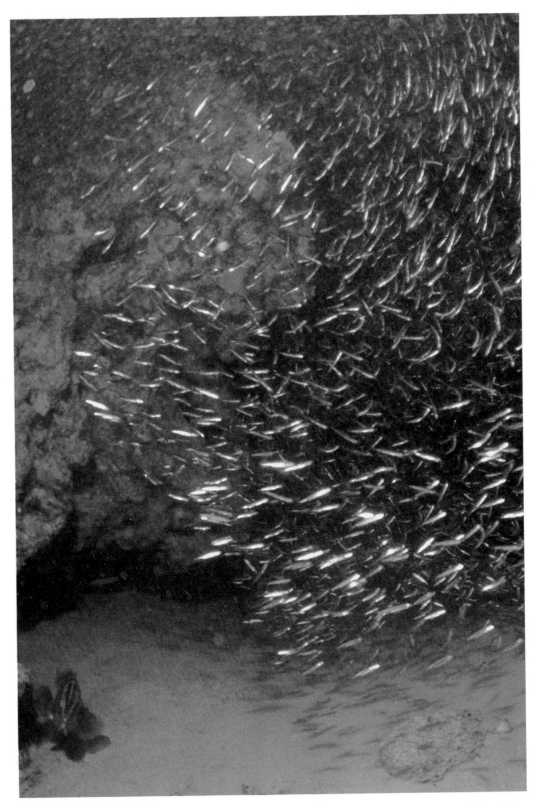

a school of silversides

# Fish schools

Many kinds of fish, when they reach a certain age and size, form into groups that we call schools. Of course, fish don't learn anything in their schools, as you do in yours. They simply move about together.

There may be only a few fish in a school or there may be hundreds or thousands. A school of herring, for example, may number in the *millions*.

A large school of swimming fish is an amazing sight, because all the fish act as one. They all head in the same direction, swim at the same speed, and stay about the same distance apart from one another. When they turn, they all turn at almost the same instant, without any bumping together or mix-ups. It's as if they can read each other's minds.

They can't do that, of course. However, it has been found that when a fish in a school sees another fish near it turn, it will turn, too, and in a split second. Thus, if a fish at the front of a school turns to get away from

danger, all the fish that can see it will turn, and all those that can see them will turn. So, the whole school seems to turn as one.

Why do fish stay together in these big clusters? It is because it helps them to survive. For one thing, they're in less danger. A single fish, swimming by itself is easy prey for a bigger creature. A codfish could snap up a great number of small fish every day if it caught them all alone. But a large group of fish seems to confuse a cod. It has trouble picking out just one fish to attack. Even though it will finally get one fish, the rest of the school will get away.

By traveling in schools, it's easier for some kinds of fish to find food. Each fish at the edge of a school is a pair of eyes looking for food. So there are hundreds, thousands, or perhaps millions of "watchers" in each school. When one fish sights food, such as a swarm of little shrimplike copepods, and turns toward them, all the others will turn, too— even those in the middle of the school who can't see the copepods. Thus, the whole school will find a meal.

Staying in schools helps fish reproduce and keep their kind going. At certain times, schools of fish will travel to special places, such as the mouth of a river. There, most of the fish will mate and the females will lay their eggs. A fish living by itself might not find a mate, but in a school it's easy.

You go to school to learn things, which is a way of helping you to survive in the world. It's the same with fish. They stay in schools to survive—to find food, to find mates, and for safety.

# Giant fish

Most of the fish you see are probably no more than a foot or two (30-60 centimeters) in length. But some fish are giants.

Some of the biggest fish are sharks. The very biggest fish in the ocean is the whale shark. This monster may grow to a length of sixty feet (18 meters). And it may weigh as much as 30,000 pounds (14,000 kilograms). That's as big, or bigger, than most of the dinosaurs were!

Great white sharks are sometimes twenty feet (6 m) long. Tiger sharks often reach a length of eighteen feet (5.4 m). And a great hammerhead reaches a length of fifteen feet (4.6 m) or more.

One of the biggest of all fish is the devilfish, or manta ray. This fish looks like some sort of weird, flying creature. Its side fins are like big, triangle-shaped wings, which it actually "flaps" as it swims. From fin tip to fin tip, a manta ray may measure almost twenty-two feet (7 m). Its broad, flat body may weigh up to 3,500 pounds (1,575 kg). Despite its name and great size, the devilfish is harmless to people and most fish. It eats tiny shrimps and crabs, and very small fish.

The bluefin tuna is another very large fish. Its bulky, but streamlined, body sometimes reaches fourteen feet (4.2 m) or more in length. It may weigh as much as 1,800 pounds (810 kg).

You've probably eaten canned tuna in a salad or sandwich. Smaller kinds of tuna, such as the yellowfin and albacore (AL buh kawr), are usually used for canning.

The big ocean sunfish seems to be all head, which is why it's sometimes called a headfish. This huge, flat, nearly circle-shaped fish may be ten feet (3 m) long and weigh more than 1,000 pounds (450 kg). The ocean sunfish has tough, leathery skin, with three inches (7.5 cm) of hard gristle under it. The skin and gristle are like a suit of armor and can even stop a rifle bullet.

ocean sunfish

# Flying fish

The big, blue and silver barracuda (bar uh KOO duh) moved rapidly through the water in search of food. Catching sight of a small fish some distance ahead, it began to swim faster. The small fish soon became aware of the danger. But as the barracuda closed in on it, something remarkable happened.

The little fish swam rapidly toward the surface of the water. As the barracuda made a quick rush, the little fish suddenly gave a push with its tail and leaped out of the water! Spreading a pair of large, pointed fins that looked like wings, it flew through the air in a long, curving glide that carried it away from danger!

People who have seen flying fish come soaring up out of the sea have marveled at this animal's ability to "fly." However, flying fish don't actually fly, because they don't flap their "wings" as a bird does. A flying fish *glides*, by holding its fins out like the wings of an airplane.

flying fish

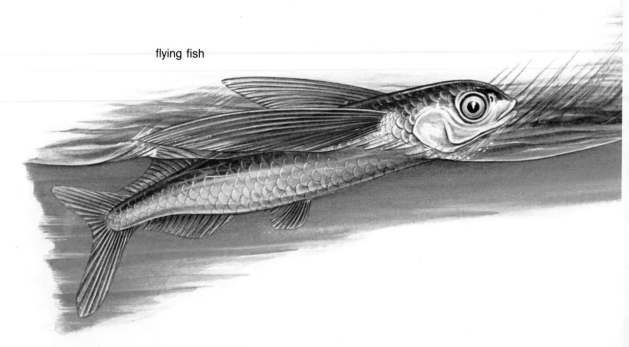

When the fish is swimming, it keeps its long fins folded flat against its sides. To leave the water, it swims rapidly and sort of kicks itself out of the water with its tail. Flying fish are able to make a single long glide of as much as 450 feet (135 meters) at a speed up to 35 miles (56 kilometers) an hour. Often, a flying fish will make a series of glides, one after another, that take it as far as a thousand feet (300 m).

There are more than 50 kinds of flying fish. All of them live in warm seas. Some kinds have two "wings" and some have four. They are rather small fish. One of them, the California flying fish, is only about eighteen inches (46 centimeters) long.

lionfish

# Ugly, beautiful— and deadly!

Some of the ugliest fish in the world and some of the most beautiful fish in the world both belong to the same family.

The ugliest fish are creatures called stonefishes. They look like lumpy rocks half buried in the sand.

The beautiful fish are creatures that are often called zebra fish, lionfish, or turkey fish. Some of them have bodies that blaze with red and white stripes. Others are maroon and white, with pale purple, black-spotted fins. Their fins and tails are like feathery fans, and their bodies are decorated with graceful flaps and frills.

But, ugly or beautiful, most members of this family are dangerous! All of these fish have sharp, pointed spines on their backs or bellies. And some of the fish can squirt deadly poison through their spines. Because of this, this whole family of ugly and beautiful fish has been named scorpionfish, after the deadly creature called a scorpion, which has a poisonous stinger on its tail.

Scorpionfish use their spines to defend themselves. If another fish seems interested in a lionfish as a meal, the lionfish will tilt itself so that its spines point at the enemy. If the other fish gets too close, the lionfish jabs at it. If any of the spines pierce the other fish's body, the fish will die. Even a person who is stung by a lionfish will suffer terrible pain, and might die.

The stonefish is the deadliest of all the scorpionfish. Stonefish often lie on the sandy sea bottom in shallow water. Should a barefoot person step on a stonefish, the spines spring up, shooting poison into the person's foot. And anyone who steps on a stonefish is likely to die within two hours!

The deadly stonefish lives in the Indian Ocean and parts of the South Pacific. Other scorpionfish are found in warm waters along the coasts of California and South Africa, and in tropical waters.

sargassum fish

stonefish

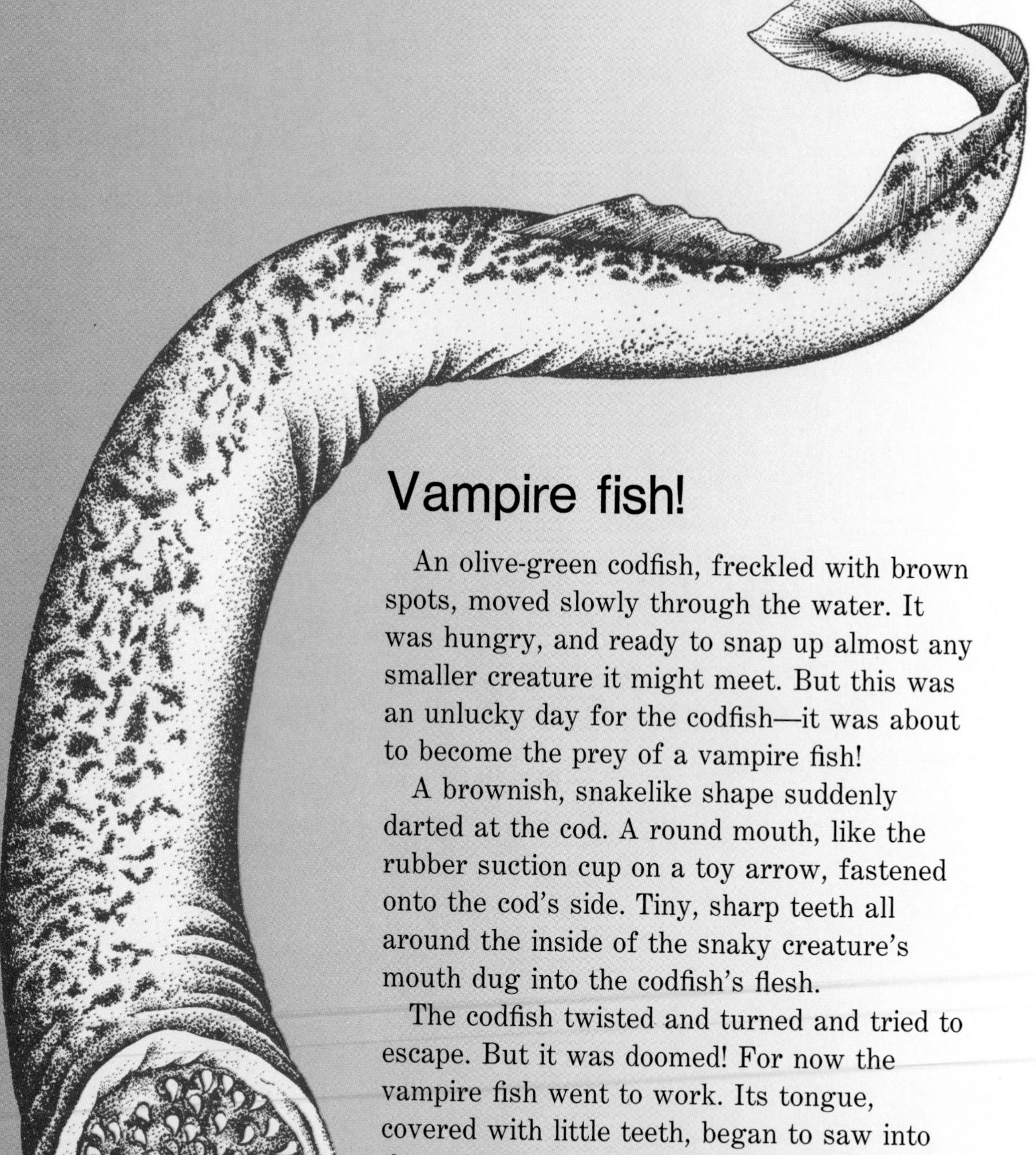

# Vampire fish!

An olive-green codfish, freckled with brown spots, moved slowly through the water. It was hungry, and ready to snap up almost any smaller creature it might meet. But this was an unlucky day for the codfish—it was about to become the prey of a vampire fish!

A brownish, snakelike shape suddenly darted at the cod. A round mouth, like the rubber suction cup on a toy arrow, fastened onto the cod's side. Tiny, sharp teeth all around the inside of the snaky creature's mouth dug into the codfish's flesh.

The codfish twisted and turned and tried to escape. But it was doomed! For now the vampire fish went to work. Its tongue, covered with little teeth, began to saw into the codfish's skin. Blood began to flow—and the vampire fish began to feed. It would stay attached to the codfish for several more days, until the cod finally died from loss of blood.

The "vampire fish" is really a creature called a lamprey (LAM pree). A sea lamprey has a snaky body as much as three feet (1

lamprey

118

meter) long, and a smooth skin without scales. And it has no jaws—just a round, cuplike mouth with which it sucks blood.

The lamprey has a close cousin that's called a hagfish. It's an even nastier customer than the lamprey. A hagfish looks more like a big worm than like a fish. It has no jaws. It gets its food by boring into the bodies of dead or dying fish with its toothed tongue. It then rasps away with its tongue until nothing is left of the fish but skin and bones!

Actually, lampreys and hagfishes are not *true* fish. These "vampire fish" are descendants of jawless animals that lived in the sea hundreds of millions of years ago, before there were any true fish with jaws and scales.

lamprey preying on codfish

# Decorated fish

Some of the most beautiful fish in the world live among coral reefs. Coral reefs are rocky formations that look like lovely, underwater rock gardens. They are found near the shore in warm, tropical seas. There you will find colorful butterfly fish, triggerfish, angelfish, and many others.

All of these fish have patterns of color that look as if they were painted by an artist. And they are perfectly fitted for life among the reefs. Some of them have body shapes that make it easy for them to swim in and out among the coral, and to hide in small openings. Their brightly colored patterns may make it hard for other fish to see them up against the coral, or may help fish of the same kind to recognize one another.

Butterfly fish and angelfish are "loners" that usually swim by themselves. Both these kinds of fish have a very small, pushed-out mouth. This kind of mouth is a perfect shape for poking into cracks in the coral to pick out little shrimps and worms that hide there. Some angelfish are as much as two feet (60 centimeters) long. Most butterfly fish are only six to eight inches (15 to 20 cm) in length.

clown triggerfish

spotted grouper

butterfly fish

121

moorish idol

The brightly colored, oval-shaped triggerfish has stickers, or spines, on its back. One spine is long and sharp, and the triggerfish can make it stand up straight. When this happens, the second spine, which is small, bends forward and locks the long spine in place—much the way an old-fashioned pistol was cocked.

When a triggerfish is in danger, it darts into a narrow crack in a coral reef and lifts its spine. This wedges it in so that an enemy can't get it out.

Surgeonfish have a sharp "knife" on each side of their body, just in front of the tail. If a surgeonfish is attacked by another fish, the surgeonfish tries to move alongside the enemy and slash it! The knife is almost as sharp as the knives that doctors called surgeons use in operations, which is how this fish got its name.

queen angelfish

clown anemone fish

blue tang surgeonfish

Surgeonfish are usually as brightly colored as most other reef fish. Some have a bright blue body, purple spots on the head, and a bright yellow tail. Others have a white body decorated with splashes of yellow, with rows of thin black stripes on the sides. But these fish often change their colors during the day, and even put on a special "nightgown" color at sunset.

There are many other colorful fish among the coral reefs. The Moorish idol has broad black and white stripes, and a startling spot of yellow on its nose. And the spotted and speckled and striped groupers have often-changing colors. All of these beautifully colored fish truly turn the coral reefs into underwater fairylands.

# Sea horses

Someone once described the sea horse as a fish with the head of a horse, the tail of a monkey, the hard, outer shell of an insect, and the pouch of a kangaroo! And this is a good description. The sea horse certainly is a strange-looking creature that doesn't look or act much like any other kind of fish.

This small, odd-shaped fish has a head that looks like the head of a tiny horse, which is why it is called a sea horse. And it has a long tail with which it holds on to seaweed, much the way a monkey hangs by its tail.

A sea horse's body is covered with hard, bony bumps and ridges. Its eyes, which are on little bumps, can be moved so that the sea horse can look in different directions at the same time! Instead of swimming by moving its tail, as other fish do, the sea horse swims by rapidly wiggling its back fin. And it swims with its body straight up and down!

But perhaps the oddest thing of all about sea horses is that the babies come out of the *father's* body. Actually, the eggs are laid by the mother, as is the case with most egg-laying animals. But the mother lays the eggs in a special pouch on the father's body. The eggs hatch in about four weeks. Then, when the babies are ready to leave the pouch, the father bends and jerks his body, squirting the babies out one at a time.

The sea horse certainly doesn't look fierce, but in its own small way it's as fierce as a shark. It is a hearty eater that needs a lot of food. And it will eat any swimming creature that's small enough to fit into its tiny mouth.

sea horse

When a sea horse sights its prey, perhaps a tiny shrimp or baby fish, it swims toward it. When it reaches its prey, there is a crackling sound as the sea horse sucks the little creature into its long, tubelike mouth.

Sea horses grow to be about five inches (13 centimeters) long. They live among seaweed, in shallow water close to shore. There are twenty different kinds of sea horses. They are found in places where the water is warm all year.

A mother sea horse lays eggs in a pouch on the father sea horse's stomach. The eggs hatch inside the pouch. Then the pouch opens and closes, squirting the babies out into the water.

# Snaky fish

Many people seeing an eel moving in and out among the rocks on the sea bottom might think it was a snake. The eel does have a long, slithery, slimy-looking, snaky body. But eels are not snakes. They are true fish, even though most of them do not have scales, as most other fish do.

There are many different kinds of eels, but the ones that look and act most like snakes are those called morays.

Moray eels lie hidden in holes among the rocks during the day. At night, they come wriggling out to hunt other fish, octopuses, and other sea animals. Morays are fierce creatures, with rows of fangs in their mouths. Their bodies are leathery, and often brightly colored. Some morays are as much as ten feet (3 meters) long.

garden eels

The eels known as garden eels have a very
different way of life. These eels are about
twelve to twenty inches (30 to 50 centimeters)
long. They live in tubes they make in the
sand. A garden eel spends much of its time
with about two-thirds of its body sticking up
out of its tube. The eel sways back and forth,
waiting for one of the small creatures it eats
to come swimming or drifting by.

moray eel

Garden eels live in large "communities." When all of them are sticking up out of their tubes, they look like a strange garden of snaky plants growing in the sand. If the eels are frightened, they pull back into their tubes and vanish from sight.

Most kinds of eels live in the ocean. But even the kinds that live in the fresh water of rivers and streams begin and end their lives in the sea. These eels hatch out of eggs their mothers lay in the sea. As tiny creatures, called larvae (LAHR vuh), they begin to swim and float toward land. When they reach the mouth of a river, they swim upstream, farther into the land.

These eels spend from nine to fifteen years living in fresh water. They grow to a length of from twenty inches (50 cm) to about six feet (1.8 m). Then, one summer, they begin to change. Their bodies get fatter, and their color changes. In the late summer and fall, the eels head back toward the sea, to the place where they were hatched years before.

When they reach this place, the males and females mate and eggs are laid. The adults then die. But the following spring, a new horde of baby eels starts moving toward the land and the freshwater streams where they will spend most of their life.

American eel

stonefish

# Fish that wear disguises

A lumpy chunk of rock, covered with patches of small seaweed, lies half buried in the mud of the sea bottom. A small fish, swimming nearby, moves lazily toward the rock, almost touching it. Suddenly, as quick as the wink of an eye, a big mouth opens up in the "rock" and the little fish is gulped in!

The rock isn't a rock at all. It's a stonefish —a fish that's "disguised" as a rock! And its disguise is so good that a stonefish probably never goes hungry—its food comes right to it! Looking like a piece of rock helps the stonefish get its food. It also protects the stonefish from creatures that might eat it.

A number of kinds of fish have "disguises" that protect them, or help them get food, or both. The fish called the leafy seadragon looks almost exactly like a clump of seaweed. And the trumpetfish has a long, slender body that is hard to see when the fish hangs head down among some coral.

Of course, these fish don't *know* they're disguised as rocks, seaweed, or coral. It is simply the way their bodies are shaped and colored. Over many millions of years, nature has disguised them in these ways.

trumpetfish

129

# Fish doctors

A snaky, speckled, moray eel lurks in the shadows of a coral reef. It is an ugly looking creature, with a wide, fang-filled mouth. And it is one of the most ferocious inhabitants of this part of the sea.

Abruptly, a brightly colored, four-inch-long fish appears. Boldly, it swims straight to the eel, as if unaware of any danger. Any moment, the eel is sure to gulp it down!

But—what's this? The little fish swims about the eel, often touching the eel with its mouth. And the eel remains perfectly still! Wonder of wonders, the little fish even swims right into the eel's half-open mouth. It spends several minutes there, then swims out again! Not once did the fierce and everhungry eel try to eat the little fish! Why not?

Well, believe it or not, the little fish is a "doctor"! And the eel is one of its "patients"! You see, over a period of time, fish pick up many unwelcome riders on their bodies—tiny worms and other creatures. These little creatures itch and irritate the fish. Fish also get sores on their bodies. So, frequently, fish with sores and lots of riders go to the "doctor."

The doctor is a little fish called a wrasse (ras). It goes over the "patient's" body, eating all the tiny riders and nibbling the ragged edges of wounds. The wrasse is simply getting an easy meal this way. But the other fish is getting rid of creatures that irritate it. And it is having its sores cleaned up so that they won't become infected.

wrasse cleaning moray eel

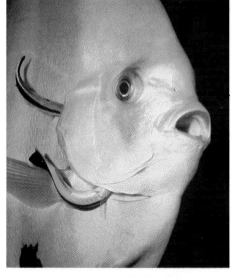

wrasses cleaning batfish

Somehow, the fish seem to understand this. Although many fish would quickly snap up a small fish like a wrasse, they quietly let the little wrasses clean them.

Wrasses often have "offices" in a special place, such as near a coral reef. Groups of fish that might try to attack and eat one another at other times, will wait patiently nearby for their turn to see the "doctor"!

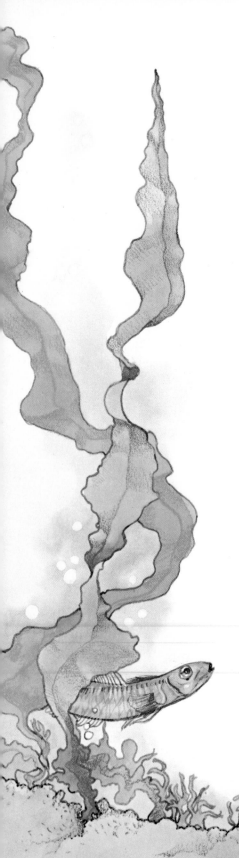

# Fishes that fish

It's a common thing for people to go fishing. Perhaps you've even gone fishing yourself. But have you ever heard of a fish going fishing? Well, some of them do! And, believe it or not, they even use "fishing poles"!

For example, there's a fish called the whiskery frogfish. Just above this fish's mouth is a thin, bony rod that sticks straight out. And on the end of the rod is a piece of skin that looks just like a fat, white worm.

The frogfish moves slowly among the seaweed. Because of its color and its "whiskers," which are long, slender bits of skin all over its body, it blends in with the seaweed. As it moves, it waves its "fishing rod" so that the white bit of skin wiggles like a swimming worm.

The white "worm" stands out quite clearly against the seaweed. A smaller fish spies it and swims toward it, expecting an easy meal. The little fish doesn't notice the frogfish hidden among the seaweed. Then, just as the little fish is about to take the "worm" into its mouth, a *bigger* mouth—the mouth of the frogfish—opens wide. And, quick as a flash the little fish is sucked into it. The fishing fish has made its catch!

The whiskery frogfish is only one of several hundred different kinds of fishing fishes. These fishes are known as angler fishes. "Angler," of course, means "someone who fishes with a hook and line."

Some kinds of angler fish are deep-sea fish. They live far down, where no light reaches and the water is as dark as unending night. These deep-sea anglers don't have a flap of skin on the end of their "fishing pole." They have a little glowing light that attracts their prey to them.

# Balloon fish

There are many kinds of fish that have an unusual way of protecting themselves when they're frightened or in danger. They swell up like a balloon!

Many of these fish belong to a family of fish known as puffers, because of the way they puff themselves up. There are many different kinds of puffers, from little ones only a bit more than two inches (about 6 centimeters) to some 27 inches (90 cm) long.

All puffers have a kind of stretchable sack attached to the stomach. They fill up the sack by gulping water rapidly. This makes a puffer swell to twice its regular size. And while it is swollen, none but the very largest fish can

puffer

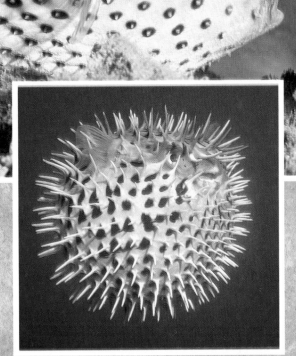

Porcupine fish have sharp
stickers. Most of the time the
stickers lie flat. These fish
can puff themselves up so
that they become spiky balls.

swallow it. Swelling up keeps a puffer from
getting eaten. If you pull a puffer out of the
water, it will gulp air to make itself swell up.

Another kind of fish that can blow itself up
is the porcupine fish. A porcupine fish has
several hundred sharp stickers, or spines, all
over its body. The spines lie flat while the
fish is swimming about. But when it puffs
itself up, the pointed spines lift up and stick
straight out.

It would be a foolish fish indeed that would
try to swallow such a large spiky mouthful.
Yet some sharks have been seen to swallow
swollen porcupine fish. What happened to the
sharks isn't known!

# Fish with weapons

A number of kinds of fish have long noses. But not just ordinary long noses. Their noses are weapons—swords and spears!

A swordfish is a big, torpedo-shaped creature that averages from six feet (1.8 meters) to twelve feet (3.6 m) or more in length. Its sword, which is really its upper jaw, makes up a third of its body length. The sword has a flat blade, just like a real sword. The fish uses this sword to get its food.

The swordfish swims along until it finds a school of small fish, such as herring or mackerel. It then rushes among them, lashing about with its sword. Some fish are stunned by blows, others are gashed and crippled so that they can't swim. Some are actually stabbed. The swordfish then gobbles up all the stunned and floundering fish that can't get away.

sawfish

The sword of a swordfish is really a very dangerous weapon. The fish are big and strong, and have been known to punch their swords right through the wooden planks of small boats. Once, a dead shark was found with the broken-off sword of a swordfish stuck into its body. Probably the shark had tried to eat the swordfish, as some sharks do, and was killed by the swordfish's weapon.

The long, sharp noses of sailfish, marlin, and spearfish are round, like a spear. These fish use their spears to get food in much the same way the swordfish uses its sword.

The sawfish has a long, flat blade that has a row of teeth along each edge. A sawfish uses this blade as both a tool and a weapon. It clubs small fish with it, as swordfish and spearfish do. But it also uses it to dig in the sea bottom for clams and other shellfish.

# Deep-sea fish

In the pitch-black water of the deepest parts of the sea live some of the strangest of all fish. Many of them have flashing or glowing lights on their bodies. Many seem to be nothing but mouths and stomachs.

For example, the deep-sea swallower fish has a large mouth that can open very wide, and a stomach that can stretch way out. Although these fish are only about a foot (30 centimeters) long, they can swallow fish that are as big or *bigger* than they are! A swallower that has just eaten often looks as if it has a balloon for a stomach!

Swallower eels, as you might guess from their name, can also swallow their prey whole. They, too, have a large mouth and a stretchable stomach that can hold larger creatures. They have a long, snakelike body with rows of little lights along the sides that flash as the eels swim through the darkness.

angler fish

A swallower eel's body may be only six inches (15 cm) long, but its thin tail stretches out for another five feet (1.5 meters) or more! At the threadlike end of this tail there is a glowing, reddish light. This light may attract prey. And swallower eels may use their long tails to catch prey, for one swallower was found with its tail wrapped around another fish.

The creatures called deep-sea angler fish also have big mouths and stretchable stomachs that make it possible to swallow things bigger than themselves. There are about ten different kinds of anglers, ranging in size from only an inch (2.5 cm) to about three feet (1 m).

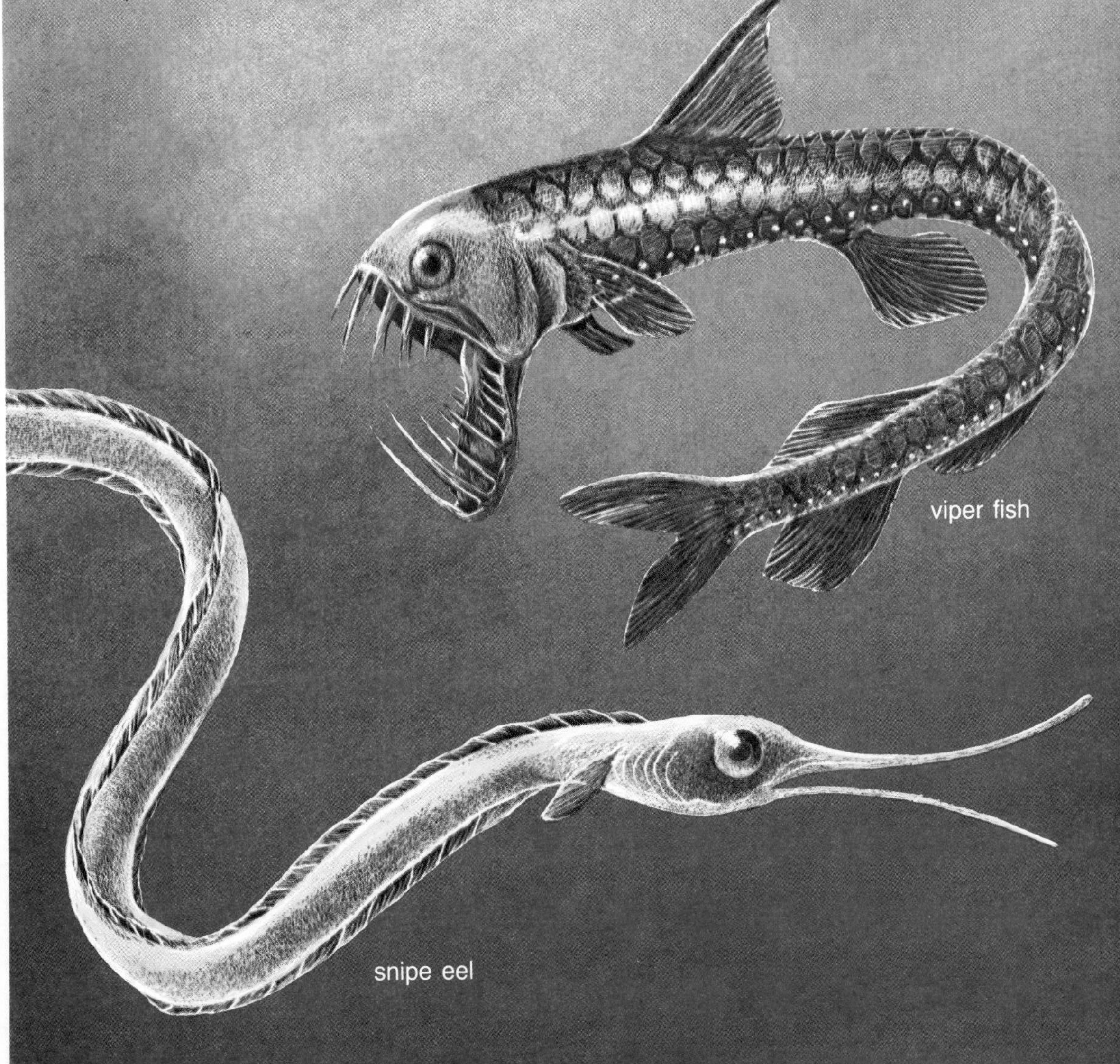

viper fish

snipe eel

Most angler fish have a long, thin rod sticking out over their mouth. At the end of the rod there is a bump that glows dimly in the darkness. Fish and other creatures swim up to this light—and are gulped into the angler fish's big mouth. Some angler fishes also have what looks like a glowing tree branch hanging from their chin.

A gulper eel looks just like a pair of jaws with a long, tapering tail attached to it. However, a gulper eel's stomach can't stretch. These creatures probably move through the dark water with their mouths wide open, so as to catch tiny fish, shrimps, and worms.

gulper eel

Surely one of the oddest of all deep-sea fish is the creature often called a tripod fish. *Tripod* means "three-legged." And that's what this creature is—a fish with three "legs." Projecting from each of its two front fins, and from the bottom of its tail fin, there is a long, thin "leg," rather like a stilt. The tripod fish often stands on these three, stiltlike "legs."

Some scientists think these fish may use their "legs" as feelers, sliding them through the mud in search of worms and other small creatures. Others think the tripod fish may actually hop along on the sea bottom!

Tripod fish, swallower fish, gulper eels, and deep-sea angler fish are only a very few of the strange fish that live in the depths of the sea. There are hatchet fish, with a body no thicker than a coin; giant tails, which are fish with eyes on long tubes, like telescopes; viper fish, with patches of glowing light in their mouth and teeth like needles; and many others. The fish of the deep sea are like creatures of another world!

hatchet fish

tripod fish

# Sharks

Most people think of sharks as being only one kind of very big, very fierce, and rather frightening fish. But there are actually some 350 different kinds of sharks. And they come in all sizes. The giant, but harmless, whale shark is fifty feet (15 meters) long. The little dwarf shark is only five inches (12.5 centimeters) long.

Sharks are fish, but they're different from most fish in several ways. For one thing, their skeletons aren't made of bone, as are the skeletons of most fish. Sharks have a skeleton that is made of cartilage, or what most people call "gristle." And a shark's scales aren't like the rather broad, smooth scales of other fish. They're like millions of tiny *teeth*! This makes a shark's skin feel very rough. In fact, in past years, people used sharkskin as sandpaper!

A shark's gills are different from the gills of other fish. The gills of other fish are covered, but a shark's gills are open. They look like slits on each side of the shark's body, just behind its head. Most sharks have five of these slits, but some have six or seven.

Most fish lay a huge number of soft, jellylike eggs. But most sharks give birth to babies that come out of their mothers' bodies, as a human baby does. Some kinds of sharks do lay eggs, but the eggs are not soft. They are enclosed in hard coverings.

Some kinds of sharks—but not most—are dangerous to humans. People swimming in the sea have been attacked and injured and killed by them. However, even the most

These pictures show the size and shape of some different kinds of sharks. The whale shark is about fifty feet (15 meters) long.

Whale Shark

Basking Shark

White Shark

Tiger Shark

Thresher Shark

Hammerhead Shark

Sleeper Shark

Wobbegong Shark

dangerous kinds of sharks will not *always* attack a person. Sometimes they will, but often they won't. But if you go swimming in the sea, it's best to be careful. Never swim at night, never swim alone, and leave the water at once, but *quietly*, if a shark is sighted.

The most "famous" and dangerous shark is the great white shark. In some places this shark is called "the maneater." In Australia, it's often called "the death shark." This shark is big, from seventeen to twenty feet (5.1 to 6 m) long. Its triangular teeth are three inches (7.5 cm) long, with edges like the blade of a saw!

Great white sharks have been known to attack humans, but they don't *deliberately* hunt for people. They will eat almost anything— large fish, porpoises, seals, smaller sharks, sea turtles, dead animals they find in the water, and garbage that has been thrown overboard from ships.

Despite its name, the white shark isn't pure white. Its back may be brown, blue, gray, or black. Only its sides and belly are a dingy white.

Another big and well-known shark is the tiger shark. It has this name because it has dark-brown stripes, like the stripes of a tiger, on the upper part of its brownish body. It, too, is a dangerous shark. It has been known to attack people even when they were swimming in very

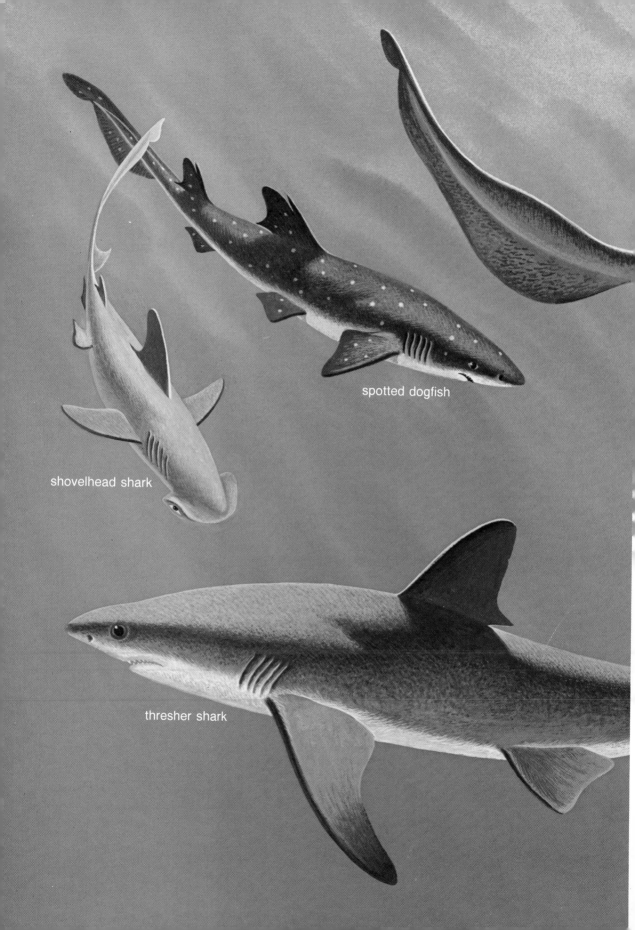

spotted dogfish

shovelhead shark

thresher shark

goblin shark

great white shark

shallow water, near shore. Most tiger sharks
are about ten feet (3 m) long, but some are as
much as eighteen feet (5.4 m) long.

Tiger sharks apparently don't care *what*
they eat. They will snap up animals of all
kinds, as well as almost anything they find in
the water. Tiger sharks that have been
caught have been found to have eaten such
things as a leather wallet, a can of salmon, a
large coil of copper wire, cardboard boxes,
nuts and bolts, and even a wooden drum.

Another big and dangerous shark is the
strange-looking hammerhead. Its body is
shaped much like the body of a tiger shark or
white shark, but its head is very different.
Where its nose ought to be, there is a kind of
tube that sticks out on both sides of its head.
Its eyes are at the ends of the tube. The tube

tiger shark

resembles the head of a hammer, which is why the shark has the name "hammerhead."

There are twelve kinds of hammerhead sharks. Each kind has a slightly different-looking head. On some kinds, the front of the head is broad and shaped like a garden spade. These sharks are called "shovelheads."

The biggest kind of hammerhead shark is about fifteen feet (4.6 m) long. It is known as the great hammerhead. The smallest are four to five feet (1.2 to 1.5 m) long.

The smaller hammerheads do their hunting close to the sea bottom and eat mainly crabs and barnacles. Medium-sized hammerheads go after large fish—and often after smaller hammerheads!

The great hammerhead eats all sorts of things. But it seems to be especially fond of the flat-bodied fish called a ray. It pays no attention to the fact that most kinds of rays have long tails with poisonous stickers, or spines, in them. The rays stick these spines into creatures that bother them. One large hammerhead that was caught had *fifty-four* of these poisonous spines sticking in its head and body. The spines didn't seem to bother the shark a bit!

The larger kinds of hammerheads are dangerous to humans. People swimming in the sea in several parts of the world have been attacked, and in some cases killed, by hammerhead sharks.

The hammerhead shark may have a strange-looking front end, but the shark called a thresher has a strange-looking back end. The thresher is a big shark, about twenty feet (6 m) long. But half that length is made up of an enormously long, curved tail. The thresher uses this tail to get its food.

When a hungry thresher sees a school of small fish, such as herring or mackerel, it moves in close and begins to swim swiftly around them. It lashes the water with its long tail, using it like a whip. This causes the fish in the school to bunch together. Then the thresher shark

hammerhead shark

charges into them, biting and gulping until it has eaten its fill.

Thresher sharks also use their tails to stun fish that are swimming by themselves. A thresher shark was once seen swimming toward an injured sea gull that was floating on the water. With a slap of its tail, the shark killed the gull, then ate it.

The whale shark, the biggest of all sharks, is also the biggest of all fish. Most whale sharks are at least fifty feet (15 m) long, and some may be as much as sixty feet (18 m) long. In spite of their size, they eat only very small fish and squid, and the tiny, drifting plants and animals called plankton. These big sharks are so harmless people can swim right up to them and touch them. They will even let people hitch a ride on their back!

The second biggest shark is the basking shark. It measures up to forty feet (12 m) in length. Also a harmless creature, the basking shark eats only plankton. Of course, it takes a *lot* of plankton to fill such a big creature's stomach, so a basking shark spends most of its time eating. It swims slowly along with its mouth open. At the back of its throat is a kind of bony "sieve" that strains the plankton out of the water.

The wobbegong is a shark that spends most of its time lying on the sea bottom, waiting for crabs and other creatures to come up to it and be eaten. You might wonder why a crab would do such a foolish thing, and the answer is that the animals the wobbegong eats do not know the shark is there! You see, it wears a disguise. It looks just like a clump of rocks sitting in a patch of waving seaweed.

Wobbegongs have rather lumpy bodies and bumpy, splotchy-colored skin that looks like rock. Around the wobbegong's head and mouth are little flaps of skin that look like bits of seaweed. When a fish or crab comes up to the "rock" to look for a worm or other small creature among the "seaweed," the wobbegong's big mouth suddenly opens up. And that's the end of the fish or crab. The biggest wobbegongs are about ten feet (3 m) long.

Sharks are usually found in warm waters. But there is one kind of shark that lives in the cold, cold waters near the North Pole! This shark is quite different from sharks such as the fast-moving white shark, tiger shark, and others of that sort. It moves so slowly that it seems half asleep. This is why it is usually called a sleeper shark.

The sleeper shark is about eight to twelve feet (2.4 to 3.6 m) long. It has a stout, clumsy body and a rather small head. These sharks seem to prefer to eat dead animals they find in the water. Perhaps this is because they don't have to chase such things. Sleepers also eat seals. But it's a mystery how such a slow-moving creature can catch a fast-moving seal.

Several kinds of sharks live in very deep water and are not often seen at the surface. One of these, the lizard shark, looks more like a small sea serpent than a shark! It has a head like a lizard, and a thin, snaky body about six feet (1.8 m) long. This shark has six gill slits, with lacy, curly edges, like frills. So, it is also known as a frilled shark.

The lantern shark is also a deep-sea shark that lives far down in the darkness. It got its

wobbegong shark

name because the bottom part of its body
glows like a lantern, with a bright greenish
light. The lantern shark is only about twelve
inches (30 cm) long. It eats small squid and
shrimp.

These are only a few of the many kinds of
sharks there are. There are also sharks called
catsharks and sharks called dogfishes. There
are swell sharks, which got their name
because they puff themselves up like balloons.
And there are goblin sharks, angel sharks,
and many others.

As you can see, a shark isn't necessarily a
big, fast, dangerous fish with sharp teeth.
Sharks are a big "family." They don't all look
alike or live in the same way.

# Crustaceans

Beetles and other many-legged creatures belong to a huge "family" of animals we call arthropods (AHR thruh pahdz). All arthropods have a jointed body, a shell, and three or more pairs of legs. Though *arthropod* means "jointed foot," it is the legs that are jointed.

There are many kinds of arthropods in the sea. Shrimp, crabs, lobsters, and barnacles are seagoing arthropods that have a special name. They are called crustaceans (kruhs TAY shunz). The name means "shelled ones."

All crustaceans have a number of pairs of legs. Most have feelers, or antennae (an TEHN ee) for touching and feeling. Some can also smell with their antennae.

All crustaceans breathe with gills. And most of them shed their shells from time to time. For a while, the crustacean's body is soft, and can grow. Then, its outer skin becomes hard and is its new shell.

Some crustaceans are swimmers. Some only scuttle about on the bottom. And some stick themselves head down onto a rock and never move again—except to wiggle their legs!

common lobster

# The gawky lobster

Many people think that lobsters are bright red. That's because they've only seen *cooked* lobsters. Cooking turns them red. But live lobsters are greenish, or bluish, or brownish.

A lobster is a rather complicated-looking animal. It has all sorts of legs and "arms" and feelers and flaps that stick out from its body. This is because a lobster's body is divided into many sections, and on almost every section there's a pair of something.

The first section has a pair of eyes, on short stems. On the second section there is a pair of short antennae, with two branches. On the third section are two long antennae.

The next six sections have differently shaped, little leglike things. These are used for crushing and chewing food and moving it up to the lobster's mouth. A lobster doesn't chew with its mouth—the mouth is just an opening.

On the next section there are two big legs that are used much like arms. Each ends in a big claw. One claw is quite heavy and has strong teeth for crushing prey. The other claw, which is smaller, has sharp teeth for tearing food apart. Not all lobsters have the heavy claw on the same side. Some lobsters are "right-handed" and some are "left-handed."

On the next four sections are the lobster's legs—eight of them—that it uses for walking. Most of the rest of the sections have pairs of paddles that the lobster uses for swimming.

Most lobsters live along rocky coasts. Each lobster has its own "home," which is a hole in the rocks where it stays hidden during the day. At night, it comes out and walks along the ocean bottom in search of food. Lobsters eat snails, clams, small fish and dead animals they chance to find. Some lobsters also eat small amounts of seaweed.

After it feeds, a lobster always returns to its hole. It is in constant danger when away from home. Even though a lobster's armorlike skin protects it from many creatures, this "armor" is no protection at all against some. An octopus, for example, can easily break open a lobster's shell and happily feast on the soft flesh beneath.

Like all crustaceans, a lobster has to crawl out of its shell from time to time in order to grow. The tough shell splits across the back, at about the middle of the lobster's body. The lobster then slowly backs out of this opening, leaving a complete but empty "suit of armor" behind.

The new shell, which has already formed under the old one, is soft. It gives the lobster no protection. Even the claws are too soft to be of use.

For about six weeks the lobster stays in its hole. During this time the new shell slowly hardens. Not until it has a new "suit of armor" does the lobster venture forth again.

A lobster has to crawl out of its shell in order to grow. The lobster then hurries off to hide until its skin hardens into a new shell.

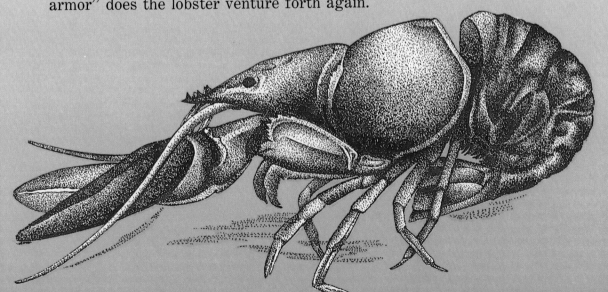

fiddler crabs

# All kinds of crabs

Someone who is grouchy is often called a "crab." That doesn't seem fair to the real crabs. There's no reason to think that any of them are grouchy! In fact, they're a big family with many odd and interesting ways. Some crabs decorate themselves, some run "races" with each other, and some even seem to play jokes on one another!

Most crabs have rather round, flattened bodies with eight legs and two "arms" with claws on them. Their eyes are usually on long stems. Of course, like other crustaceans, their bodies are covered with a hard shell.

Fiddler crabs got their name because the males often sit in front of their burrows waving one claw in the air. They look as if they are playing a fiddle. These crabs are little creatures, only about an inch (2.5 centimeters) wide.

As babies, fiddler crabs spend all their time in water. Then, they come out of the water and up onto a beach. There, just at the edge of the water, they dig a burrow in the mud or sand. Large numbers of fiddler crabs always live together in "villages."

When the tide is low and there are no waves rushing up onto the beach, the fiddler crabs come out of their burrows to feed. The wet sand is filled with tiny plants and animals carried ashore by the waves. The crabs scoop up chunks of food-filled sand with their claws and stuff them into their mouths.

Each fiddler crab has a small territory near its burrow where it hunts for food. If a male fiddler crab comes into the territory of another male, there's usually a fight! But no one gets hurt—the loser simply runs away.

Before the tide comes back in, each fiddler crab cuts out a circle of mud with its claw. It carries this to its burrow. The crab then

This hermit crab has the back part of its body inside an empty snail shell. As the crab walks along, it carries the shell with it.

backs into the burrow, pulling the plug of mud after it. The mud seals up the entrance and hides the burrow. When the waves roll in, the crab is snug and safe inside its home.

A scientist once saw a fiddler crab apparently play a joke on another crab that had just sealed up the entrance to its burrow. No sooner had the crab pulled its plug of mud into place than another crab, who had been watching, ran up, pulled out the plug, and ran away!

The two claws of female fiddler crabs are the same size. But the males have one large claw and one smaller one. The large claw is often as big as the crab's whole body. This big claw is the one the male waves while sitting at the entrance to its burrow. Scientists think that the males do this to attract females, and to signal other males to stay away from their territory.

As you might guess from its name, the kind of crab called a hermit crab lives by itself. The hermit crab doesn't dig a burrow. It lives in an empty sea shell! Sometimes it even decorates the shell by attaching pieces of sponge to it. Or, it may put the kind of animal called a sea anemone on top of the shell. Hermit crabs do this to disguise the shell.

Of course, as a hermit crab grows it often becomes too big for its shell. Then it has to go "shopping" for a new one. But it doesn't take just any old shell. It's very fussy about what it wants. When it finds an empty shell, it feels it, turns it over, and really "tries it out" before deciding to move in.

One kind of tiny crab is called an oyster crab. This crab lives inside an oyster shell, with the oyster. It hardly ever leaves. The oyster crab lives on some of the food that the oyster pulls into its shell.

There are also ghost crabs. These little creatures run about on beaches at night. They often seem to be running races with each other. Their pale gray color blends in so well with sand that when they stop they seem to disappear.

These are only a few of the more than four thousand kinds of crabs. There also are blue crabs, green crabs, rock crabs, and spider crabs. And, as you may know, many kinds of crabs are good to eat.

# Some surprising shrimp

The bandit lay waiting. He wasn't very big, but he had a pistol cocked and ready!

Suddenly, a fish appeared, swimming slowly past the bandit's hiding place. The bandit's pistol went off with a loud *crack!* Stunned, the fish began to sink. And the bandit—a tiny shrimp only two inches (5 centimeters) long—seized the fish and began to eat it!

The tiny crustacean called a pistol shrimp doesn't actually shoot its prey with a bullet. It has one very large claw, more than half as big as the shrimp itself. It can cock this claw like an old-fashioned pistol. When the shrimp snaps the two parts of its claw together, there is a loud noise.

A pistol shrimp in a glass jar once *broke* the

jar when it fired its "pistol"! The loud noise that a pistol shrimp's claw makes stuns the fish or other creature that the shrimp is "shooting." This gives the shrimp a moment in which to seize its prey. The pistol shrimp also uses its weapon to defend itself from attackers.

Chances are that you've eaten shrimp in a salad or had fried shrimp. They weren't pistol shrimp, however. They were probably what are known as common shrimp. These little animals are about three inches (7.5 cm) long. They look like tiny lobsters.

Common shrimp hatch out of eggs that are laid at sea. The young shrimp move toward shore and take up life at the bottom of bays and river mouths. They hide in burrows in the mud or sand during the day. At night they come out to feed on worms, small clams and snails, and tiny crustaceans like themselves.

There are a great many kinds of shrimp. Some of them, like the pistol shrimp, do interesting and unusual things.

For example, one kind of shrimp is a "tailor." This shrimp actually sews seaweed together to make a home for itself! The seaweed is a kind that has many thin strands. The strands grow close together, forming a kind of mat.

The shrimp lies on its back and pulls the edges of a mat around itself. Using one of its legs as a needle, it stitches the edges of the mat together with "threads" of seaweed. It can make four inches (10 cm) of tube in about ten minutes. A tube as much as a foot (30 cm) long becomes a home for a male and female shrimp.

Some kinds of shrimp clean fish for a living. They really do!

These shrimp are about two inches (5 cm) long. They live among the tentacles of animals called sea anemones. Sea anemones look like bunches of flowers growing on the sea bottom. When a fish comes near, a shrimp waves its long antennae to attract attention. The fish stops and the shrimp climbs onto it.

Most fish have many tiny worms and other creatures attached to their body. These itch and irritate the fish. The little shrimp crawls over the fish, eating all the tiny creatures it can find. Thus the fish is cleaned of its unwelcome riders and the shrimp gets a meal!

Most shrimp are gray, brown, white, or pink. But some are bright red, blue, green, or yellow. Others have stripes. And some kinds of shrimp are colored so beautifully they are called "painted shrimp."

painted shrimp

cleaner shrimp
on anemone

red coral shrimp

# The life of a barnacle

A barnacle spends most of its life standing on its head and waving its legs!

When a baby barnacle hatches out of its egg it has one eye and twelve legs. For several weeks it swims about in the plankton, eating tiny plants. A little at a time it

goose barnacles

changes, until it has two large antennae, three eyes, twenty-four legs, and a two-piece shell.

At this stage, the barnacle begins to search for a home. It needs a hard, rough surface where the water moves by swiftly. It may choose a dock, the shell of a sea turtle, a rock, or the bottom of a ship. For a time, the barnacle "tests" its new home by walking about and touching its antennae to the surface. As it does this, drops of a sort of glue begin to ooze out of the antennae.

ribbed barnacles on a snail

Suddenly the barnacle finds its head stuck to the surface! It kicks and struggles to free itself, but it's stuck for good. Barnacle glue is the strongest glue in the world!

Barnacles that stick themselves to the bottom of ships are a big problem. They slow down a ship, so they have to be scraped off. And this is no easy job.

Once a barnacle is stuck down, it loses its shell. But a liquid that flows out of its body hardens and forms a new boxlike shell. The barnacle also loses its eyes. But it still has twenty-four legs. And it uses its legs to catch food.

The legs are covered with stiff hairs. By sticking its legs out of its shell and waving them, the barnacle catches tiny plants and animals in the hairs. Then it pulls its legs back into its shell and eats the food it has caught. And this is how it spends the rest of its life.

Each barnacle is both male and female combined. So every barnacle can lay eggs. And it lays its eggs two or three times a year—ten or fifteen thousand at a time!

# Mollusks

Octopuses, snails, slugs, oysters, clams, scallops, squids, and a number of similar creatures all belong to a "family" of animals called mollusks (MAHL uhsks). The name means "soft body."

A mollusk has no skeleton. But most mollusks do have some kind of shell that gives them protection. Their shells are the "sea shells" so often found on beaches.

Some mollusks never move. But most have a sort of thick pad on which they can crawl very slowly. Other mollusks, such as squids and octopuses, have snaky arms instead of a pad. And most mollusks have a very special sort of tongue, one that is different from the tongue of any other animal. It is like a ribbon that is covered with tiny teeth. A mollusk uses its tongue like a file.

There are more than eighty thousand different kinds of mollusks. Each kind of mollusk that has a shell has its own special kind of shell. People who collect and study sea shells can often look at a shell and tell what kind of mollusk lived in it.

octopus

# A many-armed "monster"

The sun was setting over the ocean, and the sky was a blaze of pink, orange, and purple. As the big red ball slowly dropped out of sight, the bright colors faded and the sky turned blue-black. Night fell upon the sea.

On the sea bottom, near shore, a creature lay hidden among a cluster of rocks. It had lain there most of the day. Its rough, bumpy body looked so much like the rocks that no passing animal noticed it. Now, as the water grew dark, the creature left its hiding place.

The creature had an egg-shaped body, round, staring eyes, and eight snakelike arms. The undersides of the arms were covered with two rows of round, white suckers. Each sucker was much like the suction-cup on a toy arrow. The creature was an octopus.

The octopus crawled easily over the rocky bottom. One or more of its snaky arms would glide forward, the suckers gripping the ground. Then the creature would pull its body forward. It moved quite quickly.

The octopus was hunting. After a time, it met a large lobster that was also looking for a meal. Lobsters do not eat octopuses. But, unfortunately for the lobster, octopuses *do* eat lobsters.

Like a pinwheel of waving arms, the octopus attacked. It tried to quickly wrap all eight arms around the lobster. But the lobster was a fighter, and could defend itself. One of its strong claws bit hard into the octopus's soft body. The other claw clamped viciously onto an arm. A person gripped by those pincers would have howled with pain!

As the two creatures turned and twisted, the water around them bubbled. First one was on top and then the other. But the octopus was winning. Its arms were wrapping the lobster in a fierce grip. Soon, the lobster was unable

to move. Then the octopus bit into the lobster's head, injecting poison into the helpless creature. The lobster's struggles grew weaker, and finally stopped.

The octopus began to feed. After a long time, nothing was left of the lobster but an empty shell. For a while, the octopus did not move. Changes of color flowed over its body, showing that the octopus was content and satisfied. After a time it began to crawl back to its hole in the rocks.

Suddenly, the octopus froze. Something was moving swiftly toward it through the water. A long, snakelike shape. It was an eel, an octopus's deadliest enemy.

At once, the octopus squirted out a cloud of thick, black ink that hung in the water. At the same instant, the octopus shot up and off through the water. It swam backward, by sucking water into its body and squirting it out through a special tube under its head. This jet of water pushed the octopus along swiftly. To help it move more quickly, the octopus brought all its arms together, so that its body took on a streamlined shape.

Following the smell of the octopus, the eel went straight into the inky cloud. Moments later, it began to swim about slowly, as if puzzled. An eel hunts mainly by smelling out its prey, and the ink contained a chemical that dulled the eel's sense of smell. The hunter could no longer follow the scent of its prey. The eel turned away, and the octopus returned to the safety of its den.

There are about 50 different kinds of octopuses. The smallest kind, with all its arms stretched out, is only about two inches (5 centimeters) across. The largest known octopus covered a circle about thirty-two feet (9.6 meters) wide. But most octopuses have a body about the size of a man's fist, and arms that are about a foot (30 cm) in length.

The name octopus comes from two Greek words that mean "eight feet." An octopus has

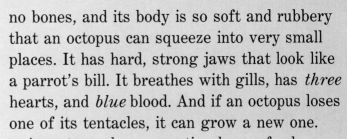

no bones, and its body is so soft and rubbery that an octopus can squeeze into very small places. It has hard, strong jaws that look like a parrot's bill. It breathes with gills, has *three* hearts, and *blue* blood. And if an octopus loses one of its tentacles, it can grow a new one.

An octopus has many tiny bags of color beneath its skin. Muscles make these bags swell up or shrink, and this causes the octopus to change color. It can become blue, brown, gray, purple, red, white, and even striped or blotched. These color changes are usually caused by things the octopus sees. And, as an octopus moves about, its body takes on the color of the sand or rocks around it.

A female octopus lays 150,000 or more eggs. After the eggs are laid, the mother spends all her time cleaning them and caring for them. She does not even take time to eat. So, by the time the eggs hatch, after about three months, she usually dies.

Octopuses are intelligent. They can learn things and even figure some things out. One octopus figured out how to take a cork out of a jar. Some scientists and divers have actually made friends with octopuses. The octopuses learned to recognize the people. Sometimes the octopuses would even reach out with an arm and stroke the people gently and lovingly! Although the bite of some octopuses is harmful, these animals are quite timid. Usually, they run away or hide from people.

An octopus seems a strange and frightening creature—a many-armed monster. But it is just another kind of animal trying to survive in a dangerous world.

# Sea arrows

The squid, or sea arrow as it is sometimes called, is a cousin of the octopus. Like the octopus it can change color and can shoot out a cloud of ink. It also swims as an octopus does, by sucking in water and squirting it out of a tube, like a jet.

But a squid is different from an octopus in a number of ways. A squid has a long, pointed body with two fins at the tail end. An octopus has no hard parts except for its jaws, but a squid has a slim, hard shell *inside* its body. An octopus has eight arms, but a squid has ten. Two of these arms are longer than the others.

While octopuses hunt by themselves, crawling over the sea bottom, squids hunt in packs, swimming. And they shoot through the water faster than most fish can swim.

Squids eat mostly fish, smaller squids, and small shrimps, crabs, and lobsters. A squid darts after its prey and shoots out its two longest arms. These arms seize the prey and pull it back into the squid's mouth. Then, with its powerful jaws, the squid chews the creature into small pieces.

Although squids are ferocious hunters, they are also hunted themselves. Large fish, sharks, seals, and many other creatures—including people—eat them.

There are about 350 different kinds of squid. Some kinds of squid are only about an inch (2.5 centimeters) long. Others are as much as twelve feet (3.6 meters) long. One kind, the giant squid, is the largest soft-bodied animal in the world.

A giant squid that was washed up on the shore in New Zealand had a body that was nearly twenty-seven feet (8 m) long. Its arms were forty-seven feet (14 m) long. All told, this giant squid was nearly seventy-four feet (22 m) long! That's as long as many of the biggest dinosaurs were! Luckily for us, these real sea monsters are quite rare, and stay in the deepest parts of the ocean.

squids and squid eggs

# The beautiful shell

Millions of years ago, the sea was full of many octopuslike animals. But these animals had *shells*, like those of snails. Today, of course, the octopus has no shell at all. And its cousin, the squid, has only a small sliver of a shell inside its body. However, there is still one kind of octopuslike animal that lives in a shell. It is the animal called a chambered nautilus (NAW tuh luhs).

A chambered nautilus is much like a squid or octopus. But instead of eight or ten arms, the nautilus has as many as ninety. The body of a full-grown nautilus is about the size of a man's fist. And the nautilus lives in a shell—a beautiful, spiral shell that is creamy white, with broad, orange-brown stripes. The shell is about ten inches (27 centimeters) wide.

chambered nautilus

Both the octopus and the squid protect themselves by squirting a cloud of thick, dark ink to confuse their enemies. But a nautilus depends on its shell for protection. Much of the time, its arms and the front part of its body stick partway out of the shell. If any enemy appears, the nautilus pulls itself into its shell. It closes the entrance with a tough, leathery hood that is formed by four of its arms.

The spiral-shaped shell of a chambered nautilus has about thirty compartments. This is why the animal is called a "chambered" nautilus. Because the chambers are lined with a shiny substance called mother-of-pearl, this animal is also called a pearly nautilus. The name *Nautilus* means "sailor."

The nautilus grows a new chamber each time it gets too big for the old one. Then it moves into the new chamber and seals off the old one. The old chambers are filled with a gas that enables the nautilus to sink down or float up, as it chooses. However, it can also swim by squirting water out of its body, as the squid and octopus do.

During the day, a nautilus hides on the sea bottom. At night, it hunts. Its arms do not have suction rings as do the arms of squids and octopuses. Instead, some of the arms have sticky patches. If the nautilus catches a crab or shrimp, it is able to hold it fast.

As it grows, a chambered nautilus adds new chambers to its shell. All the chambers form a beautiful spiral design when the shell is cut in half.

# The "spade-footed" ones

If you ever find the shell of a scaphopod (SCAF uh pahd) on a beach, you may think you've found the tusk of a tiny elephant! For that's what the shells of most of these little creatures look like. The shells are hollow, and open at both ends. A scaphopod wears its shell on its body, like a snail.

The name *scaphopod* means "spade foot." These animals were given this name because they dig their way through sand with a fleshy "foot" they push out of the wide end of the shell. However, because their shells look like an elephant's tusk, or like a long, sharp tooth, the animals are usually called "tooth shells" or "tusk shells."

There are about four hundred different kinds of tooth shells. The smallest are about half an inch (1.3 centimeters) long. The biggest are about five inches (12.5 cm) long. Some live in shallow water, near shore. Others live in the deepest parts of the ocean.

Tooth shells spend most of their lives half buried in sand. They eat tiny, tiny animals that live in the sand. To feed, a tooth shell sticks out its "foot" and stirs up the sand. Small, thin tentacles around the foot reach out in all directions, feeling and searching.

Along one side of each tentacle there are little hairs that wave constantly, like grass in the wind. Tiny animals caught in the hairs are passed along by the waves until they reach the scaphopod's mouth.

Most tooth shells are white. But some are yellow and some are pale pink. And one kind is a beautiful dark green.

scaphopods

# The life of a chiton

Imagine you're the kind of mollusk called a chiton (KY tuhn).

You have a sort of head, a mouth, but no eyes. Your body is a soft, oblong lump, with no arms or legs. Your head and back are covered with eight hard, curved shells. The shells fit over one another, like the armor worn by a knight of old. Your name, *chiton*, comes from an old Greek word that means "suit of armor."

You move by crawling on your belly, which is the whole underside of your body. Ripples, made by muscles, move along your belly and pull you ahead very slowly. As you creep along, your head and back are completely protected by your suit of "armor."

During the day, you hide beneath rocks or find a small hole that you can creep into. At night you come out to look for food. Your food is mossy seaweed that grows on the rocks you creep over. To eat, you stick out your tongue, which is covered with many tiny teeth. You rub your tongue over the seaweed, tearing off bits and swallowing them.

Or, perhaps you're the kind of chiton that eats tiny shrimps and other little creatures. If so, you catch these animals with a kind of net that grows out over your head.

When you sense danger, you push your belly hard against a rock. Your belly acts like a suction cup. It holds you so tight that almost nothing can pull you off. But if you are knocked loose, you curl into a ball so your "armor" protects your soft belly.

That's what it's like to be a chiton.

chiton

moon snail

# The "belly-footed" ones

A large moon snail pushes its way through the speckled sand just below the low tideline. The snail has a round shell that is some four inches (10 centimeters) wide. Bulging out all around the shell is a thick, fleshy "foot."

The snail moves very slowly, of course. It hardly seems possible that such a sluggish creeper is a dangerous beast of prey—but it is! The moon snail is a deadly hunter!

Some distance from the snail, a littleneck clam lies partly buried in the sand. It is directly in the snail's path. When the clam becomes aware of its danger, it closes its shell tightly. This is its only defense, for it cannot jump as some clams can.

But the clam is doomed. The snail crawls atop the clam and spreads its body over the smaller creature. The snail's snout touches the clam's shell. Drops of an acid-like liquid that the snail makes in its body spread onto the shell and begin to eat a pit into it. Then the snail's tongue emerges. It is like a rubbery ribbon, covered with thousands of tiny teeth.

Using its tongue like a file, the snail enlarges the pit made by the acid. Soon, there is a hole in the helpless clam's shell. Now the snail begins to suck out bits of the clam's soft body.

Many sea snails are meat-eaters like the moon snail. But others are vegetarians. They use their toothed tongues to rub off tiny bits of seaweed. And some kinds of snails eat dead things that they find.

Snails belong to the group of mollusks that are called gastropods (GAS truh pahdz). *Gastropod* means "belly foot." A gastropod crawls mainly by means of ripples that pass across its belly. So, a snail's belly serves as a sort of foot.

A snail has a blunt head at the front of its body. Some have a pair of eyes on the head and some are eyeless. But even those with eyes probably don't see much more than a blur. However, snails have a good sense of smell and a good sense of touch.

There are about fifty-five thousand kinds of salt-water snails. Each kind of snail has its own distinctive shell. Many of these shells are fantastically shaped and colored, and truly beautiful. Some are rounded and some are long and cone-shaped. Others are quite twisted. Still others have rows of spikes running across them.

Most snails can pull their head and foot inside their shell for protection. But some snails have such a large foot that they can't get it into the shell. And some sea snails have hardly any shell.

One well-known kind of sea snail has a shell that looks much like half of a big clam or oyster shell. This snail is the abalone (ab uh LOH nee). It is well-known because many people eat it. Its broad, thick foot is called abalone steak.

The abalone lives near shore and feeds on mossy seaweed that grows on rocks. It scrapes the seaweed off with its toothed tongue. Its broad shell, which may be as much as a foot (30 cm) long, does not quite cover its entire body. So the edge of its foot sticks out all around, looking like a ruffle on a skirt.

When an abalone is in danger, it clamps its foot to a rock. And it holds on so tight a strong man can't pull it loose. Unfortunately for the abalone, one of its main enemies, the starfish, *can* pry it loose. A starfish is able to lift up an abalone just enough to slip its thin, baglike stomach beneath the abalone's foot. The starfish's stomach then begins to ''soak up'' the abalone's body.

The shell of a live abalone looks rather rough and dull. But when the shell is cleaned, it gleams with colors. Mother-of-pearl, used to make jewelry and ornaments, comes from the inside of the abalone shell.

abalones

cowrie snail

# The "two-shelled" ones

The creature lay inside its boxlike shell, with the lid open. From under the lid, a fringe of short, thin tentacles stuck out all around. Among the tentacles gleamed many tiny, round, beautiful blue eyes—nearly a hundred of them! The creature was feeding. As water flowed into its box, it strained out the many tiny plants and animals floating in the water and took them into its mouth.

The creature's tiny eyes could not make out colors and shapes—only light and shadows. Suddenly, some of the eyes saw a humped shadow that was crawling slowly closer. And the creature's sense of smell picked up the odor of its terrible enemy, a starfish!

scallop

At once, the shell snapped shut. Then the creature made a series of hops that carried it zigzagging off through the water. Some distance away, it settled down again. It was out of danger for the moment.

The creature was the kind of mollusk we call a scallop (SKAHL uhp). There are about three hundred different kinds of scallops. They belong to the group of mollusks known as bivalves. *Bivalve* means "two valves." All bivalves have two shells, and each shell is called a valve. The top and bottom valves are connected by a kind of hinge of muscle. Life for a bivalve is like living in a box.

A scallop's shell is rounded. Usually, there are rows of ridges on it. The shell may be a lovely shade of red, pale pink, or creamy yellow. The creature got its name because the edges of the shell are wavy, or scalloped.

The oyster is a cousin of the scallop. But, unlike a scallop, an oyster can't swim. The poor oyster is stuck where it is. When an oyster is very young, it cements itself to one place and spends the rest of its life there.

If danger threatens, an oyster can only protect itself by closing its shell. Often, this does not help. A determined starfish can pull an oyster's shell open. And many kinds of snails can simply drill right through the shell.

An oyster's body is just a grayish lump. It has many little feelers, but no eyes and no way of smelling or hearing. It feeds in the same way a scallop does. By waving tiny hairs on its gills, an oyster pulls tiny water creatures in toward its funnel-shaped mouth.

Most oyster shells are rough and lumpy and not a bit pretty. But the bivalves called pearl oysters often make something that *is* very pretty—a pearl!

A pearl is formed when a grain of sand or other tiny object gets inside an oyster's shell. This irritates the oyster. So, it begins to build a shell around the object, just as it built its shell around itself.

The oyster slowly coats the object with the same smooth, shiny material that lines the inside of its shell. As more and more of these coats are built up, a round and beautiful pearl may be formed. Actually, all bivalves can make pearls. But the best pearls, the ones used as jewels, come only from pearl oysters.

The bivalves called clams lead a different sort of life from oysters and scallops. A clam has a thick, muscular "foot" that it can stick out of its shell. With this foot, a clam can dig into the sand or mud to hide itself.

There are many different kinds of clams, with differently shaped shells. One kind is a giant! This giant clam lives in the Indian and Pacific oceans. It often has a shell that is more than three feet (1 meter) long and weighs as much as five hundred pounds (230 kg). Of course, these big creatures can't move or dig as small clams can. They simply sit, like oysters, feeding on tiny creatures that float into their shells.

oysters

giant clam and diver

# Sea slugs

If you have ever played in a garden or meadow, you've probably seen slugs. A slug is a snail without a shell. It's a little brownish-yellow lump that crawls very slowly. Usually it has two "feelers" sticking out of its head. It's not a very pretty creature, at all.

But the slugs that live in the sea wear finery that puts their land cousins to shame. Most sea slugs are beautifully colored, and are often decorated with gay spots and stripes.

The batwing sea slug is a lovely pale orange. The Mexican ruffled sea slug is lime green with black and gold ruffles on its back. And the clown sea slug makes you think of a circus clown in a milk-white costume with red frills and polka-dots!

Most kinds of sea slugs live in shallow water, where they crawl about on the sea bottom. But some can swim by gracefully wiggling their bodies. Some sea slugs eat seaweed. Others eat sponges (SPUHN jehs), or coral polyps (KAWR uhl PAHL ihps), or sea anemones (uh NEHM uh neez). And some eat fish eggs.

Sea slugs are such soft, helpless-seeming creatures you might think that other sea animals could feast on them easily. Actually,

Australian sea slug

few animals try to eat sea slugs. If a sea slug is touched, a thick, slimy liquid usually oozes out of its body. And in some sea slugs, this liquid is poisonous.

Some sea slugs protect themselves with "borrowed" poison. These slugs eat the tentacles of sea anemones, which are full of stinging cells. The poison doesn't bother the slugs—they just store the stinging cells in their own bodies. Then, if any creature tries to bite them, it gets stung!

Hawaiian sea slug

# Collecting sea shells

Many people enjoy collecting sea shells as a hobby. But collecting sea shells is more than a hobby. It's actually part of a science—the science of conchology (kahng KAHL uh jee). So, if you start a collection of sea shells, you'll be a sort of scientist!

If you live near the seashore, or take a trip to a place near the sea, you can begin your collection with shells you've found. On most beaches there are many kinds of shells, all cast up by the waves.

If you don't live near the sea (and even if you do), you can get sea shells in many other ways. Common sea shells of all kinds are sold as decorations for home aquariums. They can usually be bought at pet shops. Rare and expensive shells can often be found in shops that sell stamps and coins to collectors. If you live in a city that has an aquarium or a natural history museum, you may be able to buy collections of sea shells at these places.

triton

wentletrap

lion's paw scallop

wedding cake shell

pearl oyster and pearl

Finding out what each of your shells is named, and what kind of animal lived in it, makes collecting sea shells more interesting. If you find or buy a shell and want to know about it, look for pictures of it in books. That's called research, and it's fun. Finding out what your shell is can be exciting.

On the next two pages you will see pictures of many kinds of shells. And, in your school or public library, you can find some good books about sea shells. You will probably find

spindle shells

books about shells in museums or hobby shops, too.

Put your shells into display cases, just as museums and scientists do. An egg carton is a good display case for small shells. Each shell can have its own little compartment. Bigger shells can be kept in cigar boxes. Place each shell on a bit of cotton. Make a label for each shell, giving the shell's name and the part of the world it comes from. Paste the labels near the shells.

Before long, you'll have your very own museum of sea shells—one you can proudly show to all your friends!

cone shells

conch shell

harp shell

cone shells

turban shells

volutes

murexes

cowries

auger shells

miter shells

worm shell

tooth shells

triton

tun

scallops

green turban

strombus

spindle shell

thatcher

spondylus

whelk

abalone shell

helmet shell

land snail shells

cockle shell

paper nautilus

# Jewels from the sea

People have always looked upon sea shells as beautiful, precious objects. As long as thirty thousand years ago, sea shells were used as jewelry. Necklaces made of sea shells have been found in the graves of prehistoric people of that time. And it seems that some women of prehistoric times decorated their clothes by sewing on hundreds of sea shells.

When great civilizations began to rise, sea shells were used to create beautiful works of art. Five thousand years ago, artists of ancient Ur, a city in what is now the country of Iraq, used gold, colored stones, and pieces of sea shells to make gorgeous designs. These were inlaid (glued) onto wooden chests, parts of musical instruments, and the walls and pillars of temples and palaces.

Some kinds of sea shells were prized as rare and beautiful drinking cups. One of these was the shell of the large green snail. This shell makes a rounded, gleaming, pale-green cup as much as eight inches (20 centimeters) wide. Viking kings had these shells mounted on silver stems and used them as drinking cups.

In the 1600's, goldsmiths often carved the shell of a chambered nautilus. They then mounted it on a fancy gold stem and set jewels into it. It made a truly beautiful—and expensive—drinking goblet.

In many places, sea shells were considered so beautiful and precious they were used as money. The kinds of shells called cowries (KOW reez) were used as money in parts of China more than four thousand years ago.

wind chimes made from snail shell and sea urchin spines

cup made of a nautilus shell

Until about a hundred years ago, cowries were also used as money in parts of Africa. You could buy a chicken for twenty-five cowrie shells, a goat for one hundred shells, and a cow for twenty-five hundred shells.

The cowrie shells that were used for money are about the size of a bean. To this day, shell collectors call them "money cowries."

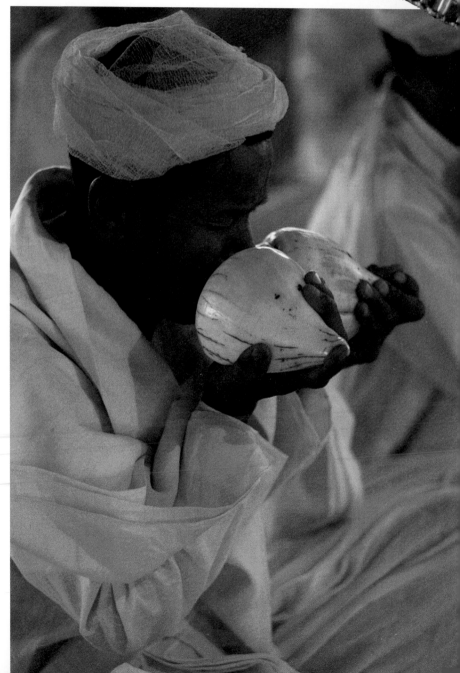

For thousands of years, people have made music and sent signals by blowing into shells. This man from Imphal, India, is using a shell as a musical instrument.

Many of the North American Indians also used sea shells for money. Different tribes had different names for this shell money. But, after a time, it was all called "wampum."

wampum belt
of clamshells

To make wampum, the Indians strung shells together, like beads. The strings of wampum were usually the length of a man's forearm, from elbow to fingertips. The tanned hide of a large deer cost about seven or eight arm-lengths of wampum.

The Indians also made wampum into belts. To make designs and patterns in the belts, they used different colored shells. The belts were used as records of agreements and important happenings between tribes.

Like many other people in all parts of the world, the Indians also used sea shells as ornaments and decorations. They sewed them to clothes, shields, and headdresses. And they wore them as necklaces and earrings.

# Coelenterates

The sea is the home of a large group of
animals that really aren't much more than a
stomach with tentacles. These animals are
called coelenterates (sih LEHN tuh rayts). The
name comes from two Greek words that
mean "hollow intestine."

You have probably heard of some of these
creatures. The well-known jellyfish is a
coelenterate. So are the little creatures that
live in coral reefs. And so is the sea anemone
(uh NEHM uh nee), an animal that looks like a
bunch of flowers.

There are about nine thousand different
kinds of these creatures. Some kinds
constantly move through the water. Others
sit on the sea bottom and hardly ever move.
Some kinds live alone and some kinds live in
large communities.

All coelenterates use their tentacles to
catch their food. Many kinds have tentacles
that can shoot out tiny, poisonous, dartlike
threads. The poison paralyzes the prey. Then
the tentacles carry the helpless prey to the
coelenterate's mouth.

giant jellyfish

# An animal
# made of water

A strange shape moved slowly through the dark-blue water of a tropical sea. It looked like a see-through umbrella. But instead of a handle, it had ragged, lacy strips and strings hanging down from it. It moved steadily forward through the water, rising and falling as it went. All the time, the umbrella shape was opening and closing, opening and closing.

A small, bright-colored fish appeared, swimming slowly with little flicks of its tail. As if curious, it swam toward the dangling strings that hung from the umbrella shape. It brushed against them.

Suddenly the fish found itself stuck! It tried to struggle, but a strange numbness was spreading through its body. In a short time, it was unable to move. Slowly, the stringlike tentacles that held it began to lift it up toward the umbrella shape—where a hungry mouth was waiting!

This strange, umbrella-shaped creature with the thin, hanging tentacles, is called a jellyfish. It is an animal whose body is made almost entirely of water. When, as often happens, a jellyfish is left stranded on a beach by the tide, it looks like a lump of clear jelly. But when it dries up in the sun, only a wet, sticky spot is left.

This watery creature gets along very well in its watery world. Upon its umbrella-shaped body are little "pits" with which it smells. And there are little eye-spots with which it can make out light. It swims by opening and closing its body, much the way an umbrella opens and closes. Each time it closes its body, water is squeezed out from beneath it and the jellyfish is pushed upward.

The tentacles and body of most kinds of jellyfish contain many tiny "bubbles" in which there is a coiled-up, threadlike tube. These tubes are filled with a poison. When something touches a tentacle, the little bubbles explode and shoot out the poisonous threads. The poison paralyzes the victim.

There are many different kinds of jellyfish. Some are no bigger than a pinhead. Others are giants, with bodies eight feet (2.4 meters) wide and tentacles two hundred feet (60 m) long. There are jellyfish with bodies like umbrellas, like bowls, like bells, like mushrooms, and like broad, flat dishes. They are all transparent, but they often glow with color—pink, blue, green, or purple.

Some kinds of jellyfish are a number of creatures joined together. One such jellyfish is called the Portuguese man-of-war. And it does look a little like an old sailing ship, or man-of-war, drifting on the water.

One of the many parts that make up this jellyfish is a sort of bag filled with gas. This bag floats on the surface of the water. It looks like a beautiful, pale-blue balloon with a pink ruffle along the top. Hanging from the bag are a number of tubelike mouths and stringlike tentacles. Each mouth and each tentacle is actually a separate animal!

The tentacles of some jellyfish can give people painful stings. And the sting of one kind of jellyfish, called a sea wasp, has even killed people!

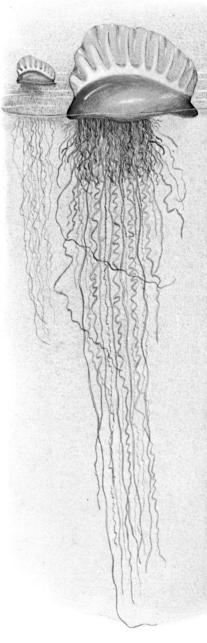

Portuguese man-of-war

# The "flower" animals

An animal that looks like a bag full of flowers and turns somersaults when it wants to go somewhere sounds like something out of a fairy tale. But there really is such a creature. It's called a sea anemone (uh NEHM uh nee) because it looks like a real flower called an anemone.

sea anemone

Like a flower growing in a garden, the sea anemone sits on the rocky or sandy sea bottom and never seems to move. Yet, it really is an animal. It has nerves, muscles, and a mouth that takes in food. The baglike part is its body. The "petals," which are its tentacles, may be milky-white, pale purple, deep red, or other lovely colors.

The anemone sits with its tentacles spread out. And woe to the fish, shrimp, or other creature that touches these tentacles. It's doomed to become the anemone's dinner!

An anemone's tentacles contain many tiny "bubbles" in which there are poison-filled threads. When the tentacles touch something, many of the bubbles burst and the poisonous threads shoot out. A small fish or other creature is paralyzed by the poison on the threads. Unable to move, it is pulled into the anemone's mouth, which is in the middle of the tentacles.

Some fish, crabs, and other creatures have formed a kind of partnership with sea anemones. For whatever reason, these animals aren't harmed by the anemone's stinging tentacles. So, they use the tentacles for protection.

A little damselfish will pick out a large anemone and stay near it. When danger threatens, the damselfish darts in among the anemone's tentacles and stays there until the danger is past. Then, unharmed, the little fish goes forth again.

This sea anemone is devouring a large grouper in the Coral Sea near Australia.

The crab is holding a sea anemone in each claw. The crab uses the anemones as weapons.

Some kinds of crabs wear anemones on their backs as a kind of disguise and protection. One kind of crab actually carries an anemone in each claw. It uses these anemones as weapons. If an enemy threatens, the crab drives it off by shoving the anemones at it.

Anemones spend most of their lives sitting in one place. But sometimes they move. Some anemones move by "somersaulting." They bend way over and take hold of the ground with their tentacles. Then they flip their bottoms up and over. Other anemones move by sliding along on their bottoms, or sort of crawling on their sides.

There are thousands of different kinds of sea anemones. Some are no bigger than a pinhead. The biggest are about as big around as an automobile tire.

# Stone skeletons

When you were born, your skeleton was already inside you. However, there are creatures in the sea that are born without skeletons—so they make their own. But their skeletons are on the outside!

Many kinds of these creatures live in large groups. Their skeletons, all fastened together, form big, stone "apartment buildings" beneath the waves! These clumps of stone are called coral (KAWR uhl). They may look like wrinkled balls, heads of lettuce, or clusters of small, stubby tree branches. Some of them make up underwater formations known as coral reefs. The little creatures that live in them are coral animals, or polyps (PAHL ihps).

A coral polyp has a body like a sack, with a row of tentacles around the top. The opening in the sack is the coral polyp's mouth. A polyp uses its tentacles to catch food and to push the food into its mouth.

A coral polyp makes its skeleton out of chemicals that it takes from the water. This skeleton, a hard material called limestone, is like a cup. During the day, the polyp hides in the bottom of the cup. At night, the polyp stretches its sacklike body upward and puts out its tentacles to catch food. It eats tiny plankton creatures.

When all the polyps in a piece of coral are hiding, the coral looks like stone. But when the polyps put their tentacles out, the coral looks like a fantastic flower garden. The "flowers" are really the beautifully colored tentacles of the polyps.

Not all coral is made up of stony, outside

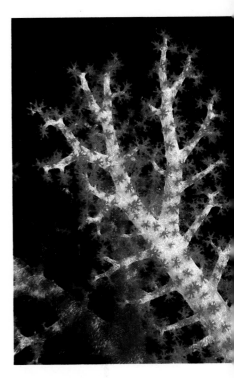

soft coral

dead men's fingers coral

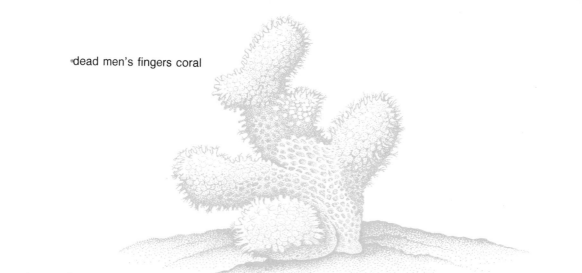

sea fan coral

skeletons that look like rock. Two kinds of coral have inside skeletons. These corals don't look at all rocklike. One kind may take the shape of a fan or a feathery plume. The other kind, called soft coral, often looks like a little tree or like the antlers of a deer. And one kind of soft coral even looks like a lumpy human hand. This lumpy coral is called dead men's fingers.

coral polyps

# Echinoderms

An animal shaped like a star. An animal that looks like a pincushion. An animal that resembles a cookie. An animal that looks like a flower. And an animal that looks like a vegetable. All these creatures that look like other things belong to one "family" of sea animals called echinoderms (ih KY nuh durmz).

*Echinoderm* means "hedgehog skin." And all these animals do have a tough skin covered with little bumps or with thorny points like those on the back of a hedgehog.

The echinoderms—starfish, sea urchins, sand dollars, sea lilies, and sea cucumbers—are really rather strange creatures compared to many other animals. Most of them have no head, eyes, ears, or nose. Some of them have "feet" and "hands." But the "feet" are hundreds of tiny tubes and the "hands" are hundreds of tiny pincers.

Many of the creatures that live in the sea have relatives that live on land, or in the fresh water of rivers and lakes. But there are no echinoderms on land or in fresh water. These spiny-skinned animals are found only in the sea.

starfishes

# Stars in the sea

A tiny, colorless ball floats near the surface of the sea. It is one of several million eggs laid in the water by a common starfish.

Within three or four days, a soft-bodied creature hatches from the egg. Like the egg, it is colorless. It looks a bit like a football, a mushroom, and a long worm all wrapped up in a ragged sheet of clear plastic! It swims by wiggling rows of little hairs on its body.

This baby starfish, called a larva (LAHR vuh), becomes part of the huge, drifting mass of plankton. It eats the microscopic plants called diatoms. Millions of its brothers and sisters are eaten by cod and other fish, but this little creature is lucky. It survives.

After about two months, the larva, now a little more than an inch (2.5 centimeters) in size, leaves the plankton. It sinks down to the sea bottom and fastens itself to a rock.

Then, during a period of about twenty-four hours, it changes. Part of it swells up, breaks off—and slowly crawls away! This crawling creature looks somewhat like a five-pointed star. It is a tiny starfish, not quite as big as a pinhead. What is left of the larva dies.

The young starfish begins a new life on the sea bottom. Much of the time it simply lies on the sand. At other times, it creeps about in search of food. Slowly, it grows bigger. Its five "arms" become longer.

At the end of a year, the starfish is about two inches (5 cm) wide. When it is full grown, it measures nearly a foot (30 cm) from the tip of one arm to the tip of the opposite arm. Its body, which is reddish in color, is covered

starfish attacking a mussel

with rows of tiny, round, hard bumps. These bumps make the starfish's body so rough that few creatures care to try to eat it.

The starfish has an eye at the end of each arm. These eyes are small reddish spots that are just able to sense light. The animal's feet are rows of little tubes on the underside of its arms. At the end of each tube is a tiny suction disk. When the starfish "walks," it stretches out the little tubes on one of its arms. These stick to the sand or rock. The starfish then pulls with its tubes to move forward a tiny bit. Of course, this is a very slow way to walk.

The starfish finds its food mainly by means of smell. And now its sense of smell tells it there is food on a nearby rock. The starfish creeps to the rock and begins to climb it.

Attached to the top of the rock is a mussel—an animal that looks a bit like an oyster or a clam. One of the starfish's arms touches the mussel. At once, the mussel closes its shell. But it is doomed! The starfish crawls on top of it. Tube feet on all the starfish's arms stick tight to both halves of the mussel's shell. Slowly, the starfish begins to pull the shell open.

The mussel tries desperately to keep its shell closed, but it cannot. The muscle that holds the two halves of the shell together grows tired. The shell opens—just a tiny crack. But that's enough for the starfish. From an opening in the middle of the underside of its body, a little sack pushes through the crack. This sack is actually the starfish's stomach! The stomach presses against the mussel's body and slowly digests it, until nothing is left!

There are about two thousand different kinds of starfish, or sea stars as they are sometimes called. Sea star is actually a better name, for these animals are not fish. They are echinoderms. Most kinds of starfish have five arms, but some have seven, or eight, or a dozen, or as many as fifty.

One kind of starfish is called a brittle star. It looks like a small circle with five long snaky arms attached to it. Brittle stars are much faster and more active than other kinds of starfish. Most of them move by slithering along with powerful twists of their arms. Some can even swim short distances.

Not all starfish begin life as floating eggs.

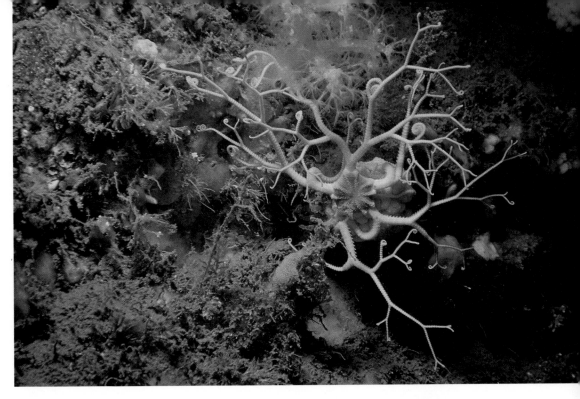

basket starfish

Some kinds, like a mother hen, "sit" on their eggs till they hatch. And some kinds keep the eggs in their bodies until the eggs hatch.

Starfish do not all eat the same things, or in the same way. Some swallow tiny snails, and other shelled creatures whole. Some feed on the soft little animals that live in coral. Some eat mud to get bits of dead plants and animals. And some eat other starfish.

Many kinds of starfish are brightly colored. They may be red, pink, purple, orange, green, or blue. Some are red with white spots, some are pale blue with red and dark blue spots, and some are white with red stripes.

One of the most interesting things about starfish is their ability to grow new arms. If an arm, or part of an arm, is bitten off, a starfish can grow a new one! In fact, if a starfish is torn in two, each part will grow into a whole new starfish!

sea urchins

# Pincushions of the sea

Imagine an animal that looks like a creeping pincushion! That's what many of the creatures called sea urchins look like.

Let's visit a coral reef near Australia. At low tide you can look down into the shallow water and see dozens of sea urchins. These are the kind called hatpin urchins. They look like black tennis balls that are covered with long needles.

The needles, called spines, are always wiggling just a bit. If your shadow falls upon one of the urchins, all of its spines will jerk upright and point straight toward you. "Touch me and I'll stick you!" the sea urchin is telling you. And getting stuck by a sea urchin's spines can be very painful!

Hatpin urchins have the longest spines—as

much as one foot (30 centimeters) long. Other kinds have shorter, thicker spines, more like nails than long needles. Some have spines that look like thick crayons, and some have short spines that are like thorns. The spines of some sea urchins are poisonous.

As you may have guessed, a sea urchin's spines are a protection against creatures that would eat it. But a great many animals do manage to eat sea urchins. Sea birds sometimes pick up an urchin by one of its spines. To break the urchin open; they fly high into the air and drop it on rocks. Triggerfish simply bite off most of an urchin's spines and then eat the urchin.

Sea urchins have round or apple-shaped bodies. Usually, they are a dark color, such as black, brown, green, or purple. Just beneath the skin, a sea urchin has a hard shell that covers its whole body.

A sea urchin's mouth is on the underside of its body. It is surrounded by a thick lip. Inside the mouth are five white, pointed teeth arranged in a circle. Some urchins can dig holes in rock with their teeth!

A sea urchin's many feet are also on the underside of its body. Each foot is a little tube with a sucking disk on the end. And in among the spines are small jointed rods. At the top of each rod there are two or three jawlike "hands."

As a sea urchin creeps along the sea bottom, its "hands" search for tiny bits of dead plants and animals, or small animals, to eat. The food is passed from one "hand" to another until it reaches the urchin's mouth. There, the five teeth chew it up.

sea urchin on a sponge

# Sand dollars

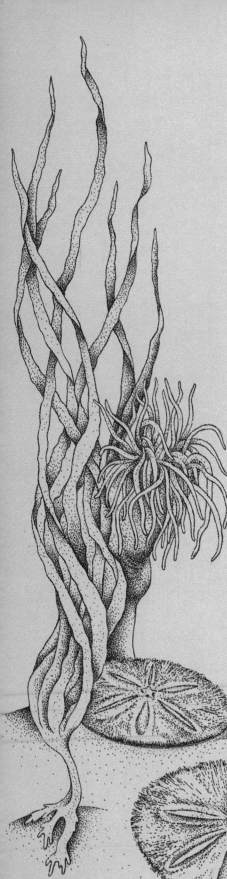

A sand dollar isn't something you can spend. It's a small animal that looks somewhat like a silver dollar or a cookie. Sand dollars are also called sea biscuits or cake urchins.

Sand dollars live close to shore. They spend most of their time buried just beneath the top of the sand. They get food—tiny bits of dead animals and plants—among the grains of sand. It's also where they're safest from enemies, such as certain snails and starfish.

A sand dollar is very much like its cousin the sea urchin. The sand dollar's soft body is covered by a tough shell. And the shell is covered by tiny, hairlike spikes called spines. Among the spines there are many tubelike feet and claws like little pincers.

To eat, which it does almost all of the time, a sand dollar waves the tiny hairs that are on all its spines. This pulls bits of food into the spines. A sticky, syrupy liquid runs from the spines to grooves on the sand dollar's body. These grooves run to the animal's mouth. So, the bits of food are carried along like objects floating on a river.

Sand dollars are small creatures, usually no more than three or four inches (7.5 to 10 centimeters) across.

# Lilies of the sea

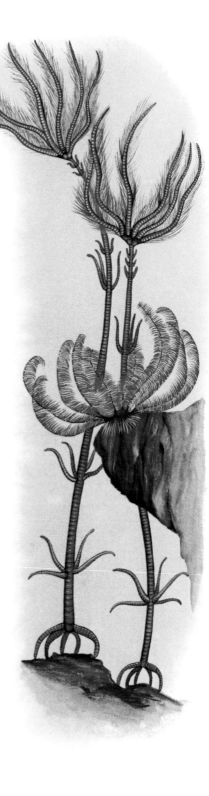

The sea lily is an animal that looks like a flower and is made almost entirely of chalk!

This sounds impossible, but it's true. A sea lily looks like a flower with lacy, feathery petals on the end of a long stem. But it is an animal. It has nerves, muscles, and a mouth that takes in food. The "stem" is made mostly of chalk, covered with very thin skin. The main part of the body is at the top of the stem. Branching out from the body are five featherlike arms.

Sea lilies live on the sea bottom, in very deep places where the water is quiet. To catch food, a sea lily spreads its feathery arms to form a kind of net. Tiny bits of food that drift down from above are caught in sticky grooves in the arms. The food is carried down the grooves to the sea lily's mouth.

Female sea lilies lay eggs that drift down to the sea bottom. The babies break out of the eggs after about five days. They are tiny, egg-shaped, swimming creatures. After a time, they fasten themselves to the sea bottom and slowly grow into flowerlike adults. Most kinds of sea lilies grow to be about two feet (60 cm) in height.

Sea lilies live in large groups, close together. Where they live, the sea bottom looks like an underwater garden filled with pink, yellow, or red flowers.

# Sea cucumbers

There's a sea animal that looks like a vegetable, gets its food by "licking its fingers," and shoots out part of its insides if it is attacked!

Because this animal looks like the vegetable called a cucumber, it became known as a sea cucumber. At one end of its body is a mouth surrounded by a ring of tentacles. The tentacles may look like bunches of leaves or flowers.

There are about five hundred different kinds of sea cucumbers. They don't all look alike or get their food in quite the same way. One kind, called the "shaggy dog," looks somewhat like a long cactus plant with stubby spikes all over it. Another resembles a many-colored vase with a bunch of small blue and white flowers in it.

One kind of sea cucumber has a flat body with rows of long, pointed "horns" on its sides and back. Another looks much like an octopus. And some look like worms. Sea cucumbers come in all sizes. They range from about three inches (7.5 centimeters) to nearly seven feet (2.1 meters) in length.

Most sea cucumbers search for food by creeping along the sea bottom on rows of little tube-shaped feet. They catch their food with their tentacles. The tentacles are sticky, and tiny plants and animals stick to them. Then the sea cucumber pokes each tentacle into its mouth and sort of licks the plants and animals off—just as you might lick jam off your fingers.

Other kinds creep through the mud, just as

earthworms dig their way through soil. Like earthworms, these creatures eat the mud to get bits of dead plants and animals that are in it. Some sea cucumbers bury themselves in mud, with only their tentacles sticking out to catch food in the water.

Sea cucumbers are slow and helpless. But they do have an amazing way of defending themselves. They turn themselves partly inside out and spit some of their insides at their enemy! While the enemy stops to feed on this mass, the sea cucumber has time to crawl away. In about six weeks it will grow new insides!

One of these sea cucumbers is stretched out to its full length. The other, at the bottom of the picture, is curled into a ball.

**Reptiles** The scaly skinned creatures we call snakes, lizards, turtles, crocodiles, and alligators are all reptiles (REHP tuhls). Hundreds of millions of years ago, reptiles ruled the earth. They started out as land animals, and most are still land animals.

Long ago, however, a number of reptiles became sea dwellers. There are now snakes and turtles that spend their whole lives at sea. They wouldn't be able to exist on the land. Yet, because their ancestors were land dwellers, these sea-going reptiles are still tied to the land in several ways.

For one thing, unlike fish and most other ocean animals that can breathe in water, reptiles are air breathers. Even though the sea is their home, they can drown in it!

For another thing, most reptiles lay eggs with shells. But an egg with a shell is designed to be laid on *land*. It would sink in water. So the sea-going reptiles that lay eggs *must* come onto the land to lay their eggs.

But in all other ways, the sea reptiles are creatures of the water. They are as much at home in the water as a fish.

hawksbill turtle

# Turtles of the sea

The biggest of all turtles makes its home in the sea. It's called the leatherback because its shell is covered by leathery black skin. A full-grown leatherback may be more than six feet (1.8 meters) long and weigh more than a thousand pounds (450 kilograms).

The leatherback is a marvelous swimmer. It seems to soar through the water, flapping its long front flippers like wings. It eats fish, squid, octopus, sea urchins, jellyfish, and some seaweed.

newly hatched green turtles

Leatherback turtles are a "family" all by themselves. But there is another family that contains a number of different kinds of sea turtles. All the turtles of this family are quite large, but not as large as the leatherback. And, unlike the leatherback, they all have shells that are covered with a hard material instead of skin.

The biggest of these turtles is the green turtle. It may be more than four feet (1.2 meters) long. It gets its name from the greenish color of its fat. Green turtles eat mostly sea plants.

The loggerhead turtle is a bit more than three feet (1 meter) long. This turtle eats mainly shrimps and crabs. The slightly smaller hawksbill turtle has a beak like a hawk. It eats plants, sea urchins, and jellyfish. Two other kinds of sea turtles are the Atlantic ridley and the Pacific ridley. Each kind is about two feet (60 centimeters) in length.

Sea turtles cannot pull their legs, head, and tail into their shell as some kinds of freshwater turtles can. The males almost never come onto land. And the females usually come onto land only to lay their eggs.

At egg-laying time, the females may swim for more than a thousand miles (1,600 kilometers) to reach special beaches where they always lay their eggs. Thousands of them come to the beaches at the same time.

They usually stay in the water near shore until night. Then, in the darkness, they all move up onto the sand.

Their shells are so heavy out of water that the turtles have a difficult time moving on land. They lift themselves up on their flippers and drag themselves slowly along. When they stop to rest, they often give what sounds like a deep, tired sigh!

Once they are past the part of the beach that is covered by high tide, they begin to dig. Green turtles, loggerheads, and leatherbacks make pits wide enough to hold their whole body. Then they dig a hole in the bottom of the pit and lay their eggs in it. A green turtle lays about one hundred eggs. Other kinds of sea turtles lay from fifty to two hundred eggs.

When all the eggs are laid, the turtles cover them with sand. Then they sweep sand about with their flippers to hide the nest from animals that would dig up the eggs and eat them. At the first sign of daylight, the turtles drag themselves slowly across the beach and back to the water.

The eggs hatch in about two or three months. The baby turtles push their way up through the sand and scramble across the beach toward the water. Often, there are thousands of baby turtles, all desperately flopping toward the sea at the same time.

Many of them never get to the water. They are gobbled up by gulls, terns, frigates, and other sea birds. And many that do get to the sea are eaten by fish. Out of millions of baby turtles that hatch every year, only a very few live to grow up!

# Real sea serpents

There really are sea serpents! However, they aren't strange, giant monsters. They are simply real snakes. They're much like the snakes that live on land, except that they spend their lives in the sea.

Even though sea snakes make their home in the water, they can't get oxygen from the water as fish do. They are air breathers, just like their land cousins.

Some sea snakes come ashore to lay eggs. But other kinds never come ashore at all—their young are born right in the water. If one of these sea snakes is cast ashore, it is almost as helpless as a fish out of water. It can't crawl as land snakes do.

A sea snake isn't shaped quite the same way as a land snake. For one thing, its tail is flattened out, like the tail of a fish. The tail acts as a rudder when the snake swims.

Most kinds of sea snakes live in rather shallow water near the coasts of Asia and Australia. The largest of them are about six feet (1.8 meters) long and about three inches (7.5 centimeters) thick.

Sea snakes eat mostly small fish and eels, which they kill with poison. A sea snake strikes at a fish, just as a rattlesnake or cobra strikes at a rat or a mouse. The sea snake's fangs squirt poison into the fish, killing it. Then the snake swallows it down.

Most land snakes live by themselves, but sea snakes seem to like to live in big groups. Sometimes thousands of them can be seen swimming along together on top of the water, basking in the warm sunshine.

# Mammals

Dogs, cats, horses, monkeys, and humans are some of the creatures called mammals (MAM uhls). They're all warm-blooded and have some hair. This is one way to tell them from fish and reptiles, which are cold-blooded and hairless.

But there is one thing that makes a mammal truly different from any other kind of animal. Baby mammals get milk from their mother's body. The milk is made inside the mother, in parts of her body that scientists call mammae (MAM ee). It is from the word *mammae* that we get the word *mammal.*

Most kinds of mammals live on the land. But there are a number of kinds—seals, walruses, whales, dolphins, and others—that make their home in the sea. Some can stay underwater for long periods of time. But, like all mammals, they are air breathers. They must come to the surface to breathe.

Whales and dolphins look so much like fish that many people think they are fish. But they are mammals—because they have some hair, are warm-blooded, and nurse their young.

sea lion

# The "fin-footed" ones

It was September, and the beginning of spring in the southern part of the world. Near a small island in the Antarctic Ocean, the water was filled with bobbing brown heads. Hundreds of animals were swimming toward the island's flat, sandy beach.

The first of the animals to reach the beach dragged itself ashore with many groaning sounds. It was an immense animal, some twenty feet (6 meters) long. Its bulky body must have weighed nearly eight thousand pounds (3,600 kilograms).

The animal pulled itself over the sand with a pair of thick, front flippers. The back part of its body ended in a pair of joined flippers, which dragged along the ground. It had a round head, with a long, curved, trunklike nose. The animal was a male elephant seal.

elephant seals

More and more of the big seals flopped up onto the beach. Before long, fighting broke out. Each male wanted his own territory, or space, on the beach. The only way to keep it was to drive every challenger away. The animals bumped their big bodies together, biting savagely. Finally one would give up and flop away to seek another place.

Later that month, the female elephant seals joined the males on the island. Each male then rounded up as many females as he could, herding them into his territory.

Seals, sea lions, and walruses belong to the same "family" of seagoing mammals. All these animals are called pinnipeds (PIHN uh pehds), which means "fin-foot." And their fins *are* simply flattened feet.

These sea mammals are very different from whales, porpoises, and dolphins. Although they spend much of their time in the water, they are able to come onto land and waddle about on their fin-feet. Whale and dolphin babies are born in water, but all pinniped babies are born on land.

All the pinnipeds live very much the same sort of life. They all eat only animals. But different kinds of pinnipeds eat different kinds of animals. Elephant seals, which are the biggest of all pinnipeds, eat mostly squid and fish, as do many smaller kinds of seals. Some seals eat mainly tiny shrimp that they strain out of the water, much like baleen whales do. Leopard seals eat penguins and young seals.

Walruses are large seals. But they are a little different from other seals in several ways. The biggest difference is that a walrus has long tusks. The walrus uses its tusks to dig clams

leopard seal

baby sea lion

and other shellfish out of the sand, or to pry them off rocks. It then apparently sucks out the clam's soft body and spits out the shell.

A walrus also uses its tusks to pull itself out of the water and up onto the ice. The walrus stretches up out of the water and jams the points of its tusks into the ice. It then pulls itself forward until it can get its flippers onto the ice. The bottoms of the flippers are covered with a rough skin that keeps them from slipping on the slick surface.

walruses

Seals can be found in many parts of the world. Some kinds live where the climate is warm, such as near the Hawaiian Islands. Others live in the cold water near the North Pole or the South Pole. Walruses all live in the Far North.

Pinnipeds have several enemies, such as sharks and killer whales. But their worst enemy is people. These animals have been hunted until there are very few left. Some kinds of seals have been killed off altogether.

# Giants of the sea

It was a bright July day. The calm sea off the northern coast of Norway sparkled in the sunlight. A flock of birds wheeled overhead.

Suddenly an enormous, dripping, dark-gray shape shot up out of the water. Its huge, open mouth was filled with what looked like a gray fringe. The big, curved body was fully fifty feet (15 meters) long.

For a moment the animal seemed to hang in the air. Then it crashed back into the water and vanished in a torrent of spray. It was a humpback whale leaping about in play!

For thousands of years, people thought that whales were giant fish. But today we know that they are mammals. Although whales look like fish, you can quickly tell them apart by the tail. Fish have vertical, or straight up and down, tail fins. Whales have sideways tail fins. Whales swim by moving their flukes, or tail fins, up and down. Most fish swim by moving their tail fins from side to side.

When a whale comes to the surface, what looks like a fine watery mist spouts into the air out of the whale's head. Many people think the spout is water, but it isn't. It is the whale's steamy breath.

When a whale is ready to dive, it fills its lungs with air. While it is underwater, the whale holds its breath. Whales can stay underwater for a long time—some kinds for more than an hour.

While a whale is underwater, the air in its lungs grows warmer and warmer. When the whale comes up to take another breath, it lets

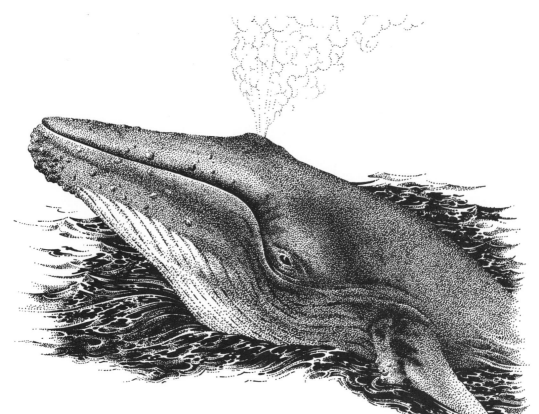

humpback whale

the warm air out of its lungs with a great whoosh. The air comes out through the whale's blowhole, which is on top of its head. When the hot air from the whale's lungs hits the colder air over the water, it makes a cloud of steam. You do the same thing when you blow warm air out of your mouth on a cold day.

Whales have no sense of smell, and most have poor eyesight. But their senses of touch and hearing are very good. They "talk" with one another by making squeaking sounds. They can hear these squeaks over great distances.

People have hunted whales for hundreds of years. So many of some kinds have been killed that there aren't many of them left. It may not be long before these huge animals disappear forever from the sea.

# Whale families

Whales belong to a group of mammals called cetaceans (suh TAY shuhnz). The name means "large sea animal." There are about seventy-five kinds of whales. They are divided into two groups. Those called baleen (buh LEEN) whales, have no teeth. Those called toothed whales, have teeth.

Baleen whales have hundreds of thin, bony triangles, called baleen, or whalebone, hanging from the upper jaw. Baleen is made of the same material as your fingernails.

These whales use the baleen to strain food out of the water. A baleen whale takes in a big mouthful of water. It then squeezes the water out through the baleen. Any food in the water is trapped in the baleen.

mother and baby
right whales

Some kinds of toothed whales have teeth in both jaws, some only in the lower jaw. They use their teeth to catch squid or fish, but not for chewing. All toothed whales swallow their prey whole.

There are ten kinds of baleen whales. The biggest of all is the blue whale, so-called because of its grayish-blue color. It is the biggest creature that has ever lived. A blue whale may be a hundred feet (30 m) long and weigh as much as twenty-five elephants! These giants live in all parts of the sea.

Blue whales eat tiny shrimplike animals called krill that are part of the plankton. It takes about two tons of krill to fill a blue whale's stomach! Krill swim in huge swarms near the surface of the water. The whale swims through the krill, sucking water into its mouth. It then squirts the water out and swallows the krill trapped in its baleen.

The second largest whale, the fin whale, is also a baleen whale. A fin whale may be as much as eighty feet (24 m) long. Its body is grayish-black, with a white underside and a white patch on the upper jaw. These slender, graceful whales are fast swimmers.

Another baleen whale is the black right whale, usually called simply a right whale. Its skin is black. About sixty feet (18 m) long, it is fatter than the blue or fin whale. It has a huge head and a sort of bony lump called a "bonnet" on its nose.

The bowhead whale looks much like a right whale, but has no "bonnet." It also has a patch of white on the end of its lower jaw. This whale has the longest baleen of any of the baleen whales. Its baleen may grow to a length of thirteen feet (4 m).

Bowheads are about sixty feet (18 m) long. They do not migrate, or move about, as the other baleen whales do. They spend most of their time in the Arctic Ocean.

The humpback whale is also a baleen whale. In spite of its name, it does not have a hump on its back. It grows to a length of fifty feet (15 m). One of the most active and playful of all whales, humpbacks often leap clear out of the water, almost turning somersaults. They also often "stand" on their heads in the water, waving their tails rapidly back and forth and sending clouds of spray into the air.

The smallest baleen whales are the minke and the pygmy right whale. The minke, about thirty feet (9 m) long, lives in all the seas.

The pygmy right, no more than twenty feet (6 m) long, stays south of the equator.

The biggest of the toothed whales is the dark-gray, square-headed sperm whale. It is about sixty feet (18 m) long. These whales live mainly in the warmer seas. They often dive to great depths to find their favorite food, squid and cuttlefish.

Big sperm whales will apparently attack giant squid. Many of these whales have been seen with scars made by the powerful arms of the squid. A sperm whale forty-seven feet (14 m) long was once found with a squid thirty-four feet (10 m) long in its stomach!

There is a family of toothed whales called beaked whales. They were given this name because they have long, rounded, beaklike snouts.

The biggest beaked whale is the giant bottle-nosed whale. It is about forty feet (12 m) long. Its smaller cousin, the bottle-nosed whale, is about thirty feet (9 m) long. These whales, too, eat mostly cuttlefish and squid.

Probably the strangest of all whales is the creature known as the narwhal—the whale with a horn on its nose! The horn is actually a twisted tooth, sometimes nine feet (2.7 m) long. It sticks straight out from the whale's upper jaw. Only the male has this long tusk. Scientists are not sure what it is used for.

Narwhals are grayish on top and whitish underneath, with dark spots over the entire body. These whales are about fifteen feet (5 m) long, not counting the tusk. Narwhals live in small groups in the cold Arctic seas. They eat squid, shrimp, crabs, and fish.

male narwhal

# Dolphins and porpoises

The dolphin (DAHL fuhn) and the porpoise (PAWHR puhs) are really small whales. Both belong to the large group of whales called toothed whales.

Most people can't tell a dolphin from a porpoise. But there is an easy way to tell them apart. The snout of a dolphin forms a stubby, rounded beak. A porpoise does not have a beak. Also, dolphins are much more playful than porpoises. They often leap up out of the water, which porpoises seldom do.

There are seven kinds of porpoises. All are smaller than most dolphins. The common porpoise is about five feet (1.5 m) long. Porpoises live in all parts of the world and eat mostly fish.

There are about thirty kinds of dolphins. The best-known is the bottle-nosed dolphin. It is more than eight feet (2.4 meters) long, with a gray body and a rounded forehead. Its beaked mouth seems to be always smiling.

Bottle-nosed dolphins are smart and are easily trained to do tricks. They often put on shows at aquariums and zoos. A bottle-nosed dolphin named Flipper was once the star of a television series.

Bottle-nosed dolphins live in all parts of the world, usually in coastal waters. They eat mostly small fish.

The common dolphin is especially well liked by sailors. Schools of these dolphins often follow ships. For hundreds of years, sailors have believed that they are a sign of a happy voyage. The animals actually seem to enjoy putting on a show. They will dive in and out

spotted dolphins

of the water and even "dance" on the surface
on their tail fins.

Common dolphins are about seven feet
(2.1 m) long, with black or dark-gray backs
and white undersides. They live in warm
parts of the ocean and eat mostly fish.

Another kind of dolphin is called Risso's
dolphin. It is about thirteen feet (4 m) long.
Unlike their relatives, Risso's dolphins don't
have much of a beak. They eat mostly squid
and cuttlefish, rather than fish.

One Risso's dolphin became quite famous.

killer whale

porpoise

T. BOYER.

For twenty-four years, this dolphin escorted ships through Pelorus Sound, near New Zealand. A favorite with travelers, it became known as "Pelorus Jack."

One kind of dolphin—the killer whale—has a bad reputation. Killer whales are big creatures, as much as thirty feet (9 m) long, with a black back and a white underside. They live in groups in all parts of the ocean.

Until a very short time ago, it was believed that killer whales were vicious, bloodthirsty beasts that would attack and eat anything— even people! Now we know that killer whales eat mostly fish and squid, although they will also eat dolphins, porpoises, and small seals.

Scientists have also found that killer whales are very intelligent animals. They can be tamed, and will even do tricks, like other dolphins. They really don't deserve their name or their bad reputation!

Dolphins can make a number of different sounds, such as squeaks, whistles, clicks, and quacks. They do this by blowing air out of the blowhole, or nostril, on top of the head. The dolphins communicate with each other by means of these sounds. A young dolphin that has been separated from its mother will make a noise that brings her hurrying to it.

Scientists think that dolphins can also make sounds that imitate human speech. However, they "speak" so rapidly, and with such high sounds, that it is difficult to understand them. But dolphins are so intelligent that some scientists think they can be taught how to *really* talk with people—not just imitate the sounds of words, as a parrot does, but actually hold conversations!

# Sponges, sea squirts, and worms

The sea animals you'll read about on the next few pages aren't related to one another. They belong to different groups of animals.

One group that you may know is the sponges. Sponges all belong to one big "family" called poriferans (paw RIHF uhr uhnz). The name means "having holes." Sponges are strange creatures that look more like plants than animals. For a long time, people thought they were plants!

Another group is made up of creatures called sea squirts. Their scientific name is tunicates (TOO nuh kihts), which means "dressed in a tunic." A tunic is a short gown or coat. And the small, odd-looking tunicates do have a thick, leathery coat of skin.

The third group is made up of worms. There are a great many kinds of worms in the sea. Some are like land worms, but others are very different. There isn't just one "family" of worms. There are a number of different families.

Poriferans, tunicates, and worms play an important part in the life of the sea.

sponges

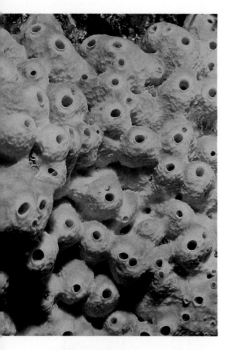

yellow sponges

elephant-ear sponges

# An animal that never moves

Sitting on the sea bottom is an object that looks like a black, lumpy ball. It never moves. It cannot see, hear, or smell. It has no head or mouth, no nerves, muscles, heart, or stomach. Yet, it is an animal—the animal called a sponge.

You may have thought a sponge was a piece of rough, colored plastic used for washing things. But these are man-made sponges, named after the sea animal. You see, for thousands of years, people used the skeletons of real sponges for washing things. The skeletons are soft and hold lots of water. People called them sponges, after the animals that once lived in them. When pieces of colorful plastic came into use, people called them sponges, too.

A sponge has no tentacles for catching food. It doesn't even have a mouth for eating. It simply *strains* its food out of the water. A sponge's body is filled with many tiny holes, so water goes right through it. Tiny plants and animals in the water are trapped inside the sponge and digested.

There are about five thousand different kinds of sponges. Some are like lumpy balls. Some are clusters of fat tubes. Some look like big vases or bowls.

Some sponges begin life as tiny eggs in a grown-up sponge's body. The eggs are carried outside by the water that goes through the grown-up. But sponges also grow little "buds" that break off and become new, small sponges.

# Sea squirts

Did anyone ever call you a "little squirt"? They were calling you after a little creature that lives in the sea—the sea squirt.

A sea squirt may look like two tubes joined together at the sides. It may look like a lumpy vase with two openings. Or, it may look like a ball with two little nozzles sticking up out of it.

These odd-looking animals spend most of their lives sitting in sand, or attached to a rock or other solid object. All they do, day in and day out, is suck in water through one opening—and squirt it out through another! That's how they get their food. They digest tiny plants, animals, and bits of food that are in the water they suck in.

Sea squirts begin life as tiny creatures that look much like tadpoles—baby frogs. They hatch out of eggs that grown-up sea squirts put into the water. The babies swim about for a time. But in a few days they lose their tadpole shape and sink to the bottom. They attach themselves head first to a rock, sea shell, or other hard object, and never move again. They grow into adults.

Some kinds of sea squirts have been named after fruits and other objects that they somewhat resemble. The sea peach is a sea squirt that looks somewhat like a peach. The sea grape resembles a grape. And the sea egg looks like a green egg.

Many sea squirts live by themselves. Other sea squirts live in small groups. Still other sea squirts live in large colonies, all joined together.

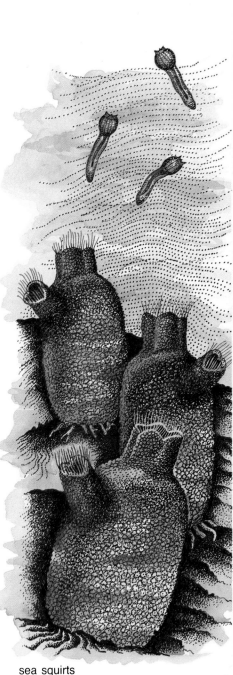

sea squirts

ribbon worm

# Sea-going worms

Flatworms, ribbon worms, bristle worms, worms that look like feather dusters—the sea is simply full of all kinds of worms!

Many ocean flatworms look like leaves that have been painted with bright colors or gay stripes. They are from one to two inches (2.5–5 centimeters) long. They glide over the sea bottom in search of prey such as oysters or feather-duster worms.

Some of the worms called ribbon worms do look much like long, colorful pieces of ribbon. These worms have tubelike "noses" that can

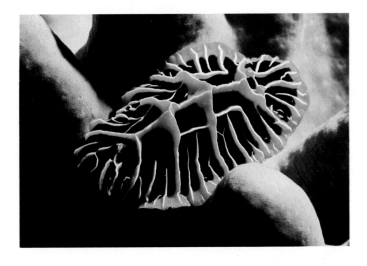

flatworm

feather-duster worm

be pushed out to seize prey, such as smaller worms. The "nose" coils around the prey and gives off a sticky slime. This holds the creature fast as it is pulled into the ribbon worm's mouth. Some ribbon worms are less than one inch (2.5 c) long. Others are as much as ninety feet (27 meters) in length.

Bristle worms have rows of bristles running along each side of their body. They use the bristles for creeping, swimming, digging, and fighting. They have groups of tentacles on each side of the head, and sharp, beaklike jaws that can tear smaller creatures to pieces.

Feather-duster worms have dozens of feathery tentacles on their heads. The worms build long tubes around themselves with a slime that comes out of their bodies. The tube is fastened to the sea bottom and the worm lives in it. The worm sticks its tentacles out of the tube to catch tiny plants and animals. When it does this, it looks rather like a feather duster. The tentacles look like the feathers, and the tube looks like the handle.

# Birds

You might mistake an eel for a snake, or think of a whale as a fish. But no one can mistake a bird for any other kind of animal. Birds are the *only* animals that have feathers. And all birds have wings, a bill, and two legs.

Most people think of birds as flying animals that live on land, in trees. However, there are birds that *can't* fly, but that can swim as well as a fish! There are birds that soar above water, thousands of miles from any land. There are even birds that sleep on the sea, and drink seawater! These are all sea birds.

No birds actually live at sea all the time. But there are birds that spend a great deal of time in the water. And there are other birds that spend most of their lives flying above the water. These birds are as much a part of the life of the sea as a shark or a hawksbill turtle.

Sea birds, like all birds, lay eggs that have hard shells. Such eggs must be laid on land. So at times, perhaps once every year or two, all sea birds go onto land to mate and lay their eggs. But for many, this is the only time they ever visit the land.

sooty albatross

herring gull

# Wings over the water

Far out over the southern sea, thousands of miles from the nearest land, a great, graceful bird soars in the sky. The bird is a wandering albatross (AL buh traws). It has the longest wings of any bird in the world. From tip to tip, its spread wings are nearly twice as long as a tall person's body! On these long, slender wings, the albatross can glide and soar above the tossing water for hours without resting.

When the albatross must rest, it glides down to the water, folds its wings, and floats upon the sea. When it is hungry, it eats floating dead creatures, as well as fish and squid that swim near the surface. When it is thirsty, it drinks seawater. Like most sea birds, it has a special part in its bill that takes the salt out of the water.

The sea is the albatross's true home. Only once every two years will it go onto land. There, it finds a mate and helps to hatch an egg. Then it goes back to the skies over the open sea.

Fulmars, petrels, and shearwaters are other birds that make the sea their home. Most of these birds get their food as albatrosses do. But some, such as diving petrels, dive into the sea to capture their food.

Storm petrels, also called stormy petrels, are the tiniest of all sea birds. They are only about six inches (15 centimeters) long. Scarcely able to walk on land, they spend months at sea. They often fly so close to the sea's surface that they touch it with their feet—and seem to be walking on the water.

The birds called gannets and boobies spend a lot of time over and on the sea. But they seldom go far from land. They catch fish by diving at terrific speed from high in the air. They hit the water with a *smack* that sends up a high splash. These birds swallow their fish underwater, instead of bringing them up to eat as most birds do.

Storm petrels often fly so close to the sea their feet touch it. Then, they look as if they are walking on the water.

Sea birds such as cormorants, pelicans and frigate birds get their food from the sea but live on land. For some of them, the sea is a dangerous place. A frigate bird will swoop close to the water to catch a flying fish in midair, but it dares not land on the water. If it does, it will die, for it cannot get into the air again.

The bird most people think of as a sea bird is the one often called a sea gull. Some kinds of gulls do live near the sea, and get food from the sea, but they never fly far from land. Sailors know they're near land when they see gulls soaring overhead. So, for sailors, gulls are a sign of land rather than of the sea.

# Wings under the water

We think of birds as creatures of the air. So it's always a little surprising to learn that some birds can't fly. But have you ever heard of a bird that can swim like a fish and stay underwater for more than an hour?

This champion underwater swimming bird is the penguin. You may have thought of penguins as land birds that waddle about the snowy land near the South Pole—but they are really sea birds. Some kinds of penguins often stay at sea for months at a time!

Penguins can't fly. Long ago, their wings developed into flippers, like the flippers of a sea turtle. With their flippers and fish-shaped bodies, penguins are marvelous swimmers. Underwater, some kinds of penguins can swim faster than most people can run.

Penguins catch all their food in the water. They feed on fish, squid, and small crabs, as well as the same tiny, shrimplike creatures that some whales eat. Like most sea birds, they can drink salty seawater. A special part in the bill takes the salt out of the water.

There are a number of different kinds of penguins. All of them live in the southern part of the world. Most penguins are rather large. The biggest is the emperor penguin. It may stand as much as four feet (1.2 meters) high—about the size of a seven-year-old child. One of the smallest—the Galapagos penguin —is about twenty inches (50 centimeters) tall.

Penguins are safe when they are on land. But in the water, they are always in danger. For penguins are often eaten by sharks, killer whales, and leopard seals.

# Strange
# stories
# of the sea

# The mermaids

'Twas a Friday morn when we set sail,
And we were not far from the land,
When the captain spied a lovely mermaid
With a comb and a glass in her hand.

Probably the oldest of all the legends of the sea are those about mermaids. For thousands of years, people in almost every country in the world have told stories of these creatures—women from the waist up, but fish from the waist down!

Mermaids were said to live in gleaming, pearly caves at the bottom of the sea. But they often swam up to the top of the water to sit on a rock in the sunlight. There they would comb their long, lovely golden hair with a comb made of fishbone and admire themselves in a glass, or mirror. Mermaids were supposed to be marvelously beautiful, and able to charm young sailors into leaping into the sea to join them.

Up to about a hundred years ago, many people believed in mermaids. A great many sailors, as well as people walking along seashores, claimed to have seen these beautiful fish-women. Even some honest and intelligent people reported seeing them.

But there couldn't be such a creature as a mermaid. It simply isn't possible to have a creature that is half human and half fish.

Scientists think they know how mermaid legends first started. Long, long ago, many people, especially fishermen and sailors, worshipped gods that were supposed to be half fish and half human. So the idea of such creatures became common. And there are certain kinds of white-furred seals that often sun themselves on rocks. From a distance, these animals do look a little like humans with fishlike tails. Most of the "mermaids" that people thought they saw were probably just seals sunning themselves.

# Ghost ships

Even though it was early afternoon, the sky was midnight dark. Jagged bolts of white lightning flashed through the blackness. A roaring, rushing wind churned the water into great waves.

The helmsman of the merchant ship stood with his feet braced against the deck, his hands tight on the wheel. He wasn't particularly worried, for he had sailed through many a fierce storm. He glanced out at the wild sea, thinking that at any moment a torrent of rain would fall.

Suddenly, out of the darkness, another ship appeared. It moved past swiftly, but so close the helmsman could make out every detail. It was an old-fashioned ship, such as he had seen only in pictures. The crewmen, dressed in odd, old-fashioned clothes, moved slowly and stiffly. Their faces were white and expressionless. Then the ship swept past, vanishing into the black of the gathering storm.

The helmsman's mouth was open in shocked surprise. "Heaven protect me!" he whispered to himself. "I've seen the ghost ship! I've seen the *Flying Dutchman!*"

According to legend, the *Flying Dutchman* must sail the seas forever, manned by a crew of ghosts. It was cursed because of its captain. One story has it that he swore a terrible curse that he would sail round the Cape of Good Hope, in spite of storms, if it took till his dying day. According to another tale, he is being punished for having killed a man on his ship.

The *Flying Dutchman* is the most famous ghost ship, but it isn't the only one. There are others in many parts of the world. Like the *Flying Dutchman*, most ghost ships are supposedly seen only during storms.

# The terrible kraken!

For thousands of years, sailors of many European lands told tales of giant octopuses —octopuses so enormous they could wrap their arms about a ship and drag it beneath the water! These giants were horrible to see, so it was said. Their great, staring eyes were the size of dinner plates. Their arms were twenty feet (6 meters) or more in length,

thick as tree trunks. And their bodies were dark green or bright red.

This creature became known as a kraken. The name comes from a Norwegian word meaning "twisted." Perhaps it got this name because sailors who claimed to have seen it thought that its many wiggling, writhing arms give it a twisted look.

But had anyone really seen it? For a long time, many learned men doubted that such a creature existed. They felt it was just another "sea monster" story, such as sailors tell.

But as more and more ships sailed the seas, people learned that the tales of the kraken were at least partly true! There *were* giant octopuses and squids living in the sea.

In the year 1861, a French warship fought a battle against a giant squid that may have been as much as sixty feet (18 meters) long. The squid was finally killed with a cannonball.

Other ships also had encounters with these giant creatures. And several dead "krakens" were found washed ashore.

One giant squid, washed ashore in New Zealand, was nearly seventy-four feet (22 meters) long! And parts of huge arms found in the stomachs of whales are evidence that there may be bigger squids and octopuses.

So, the old legends of the kraken, that many people thought were fables, are based on fact!

# Sea gods

Most people of long ago believed that the sea was ruled by a great god or spirit. The sailors of many ancient lands worshipped sea gods and prayed to them for protection.

The sea god of the ancient Greeks was named Poseidon (puh SY duhn). The Greeks believed he lived at the bottom of the Aegean Sea, in a magnificent golden palace.

When Poseidon left his palace to travel over the sea, he rode in a bronze chariot drawn by horses with golden manes. When he was in a good mood, the water parted for his chariot and the sea was calm. But if he were angry, his journey would cause a storm to rage over the sea.

The Romans adopted their sea god from the Greeks. But in Roman myths he is called Neptune (NEHP toon). Like Poseidon, Neptune was also the god of horses and earthquakes.

The people of ancient Libya, on the coast of North Africa, also had a sea god. Their god of the sea had the body of a man from the waist up and the body of a fish from the waist down. For some reason, the ancient Greeks borrowed this Libyan god and said he was the son of Poseidon. They called him Triton (TRY tuhn). The idea of mermaids and mermen, creatures that are half human and half fish, probably started with Triton.

The sea god of the early people of Ireland was Manannán. Like Poseidon, Manannán had the shape of a human. He wore a cloak that had all the colors of the sea. He owned a horse that could run on land or water. And he had a boat named Ocean-Sweeper, which

obeyed his thoughts and would go wherever
he told it to. The people of Ireland called the
white-tipped ocean waves, "the horses of
Manannán."

A little island in the Irish Sea, halfway
between Ireland and England, was thought to
be Manannán's throne. Today, that island is
known as the Isle of Man. It is named after
the ancient Irish god of the sea.

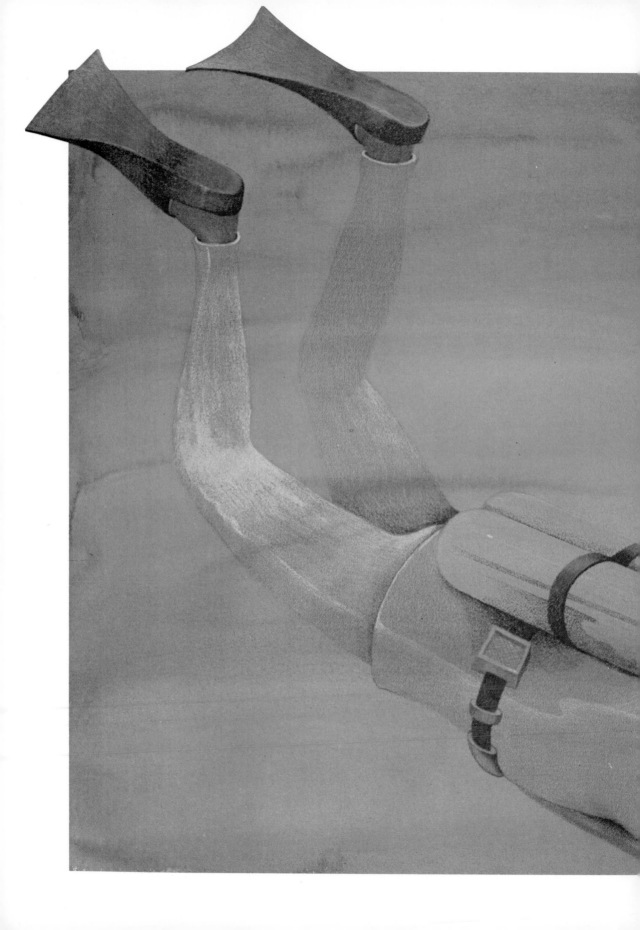

# People who work on the sea

A lobster fisher empties a
lobster pot. A pot is a trap
made of wood or metal slats.

The fishers on this ship are hauling in a large catch of tuna. The tuna will be processed and sold fresh or canned.

People who fish for a living spend a great deal of time on the water. Some work on huge "factory ships." Others work in small boats. Usually, they go after one kind of fish or shellfish. These deck hands are working with freshly caught shrimp.

Many people have jobs on cruise ships. These cooks have
prepared beautiful dishes for the passengers.

The navigator on a cruise ship
uses computers, charts, and
special instruments to plot the
ship's course.

An underwater photographer uses a waterproof light and camera
to take pictures of different kinds of coral in a coral reef.
The pictures may be used in books and magazines.

The Navy offers many careers, both at sea and on land. People aboard ships do all kinds of tasks above and below the deck. Sometimes sailors spend many months at sea. Their ship is refueled at sea by another ship.

Men and women in the Coast Guard help protect people on the sea. The Coast Guard goes to the rescue of people on sinking ships, or on airplanes that crash into the sea.

Marine geologists study the land beneath the sea. Their work helps people learn more about the world. Their work is also important because the land under the sea is a vast source of valuable minerals. This marine geologist is using an underwater drill to remove a sample of coral from the ocean.

An oceanographer studies the sea itself—the chemicals that make up seawater, the currents that flow through the sea, the effects of tides, and so on. Oceanographers spend much time at sea, often diving beneath the surface. They also do a great deal of laboratory work ashore.

A scientist in a diving suit called the *Wasp* collects plants and animals from the ocean floor.

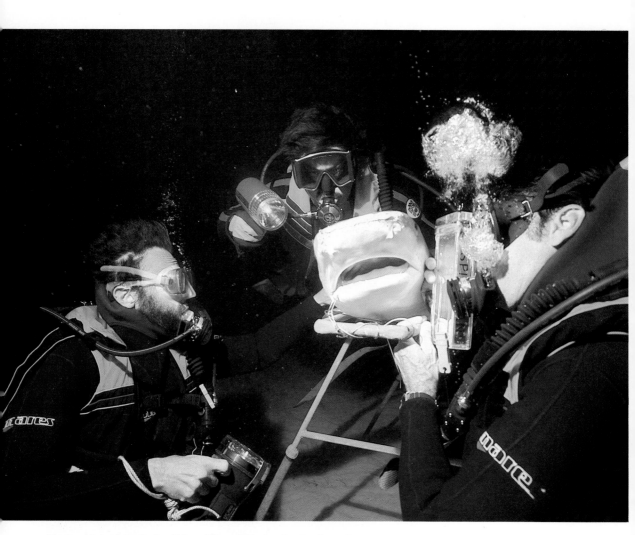

Marine biologists study all the different kinds of animals and plants in the sea. They learn how each kind of creature gets its food, defends itself, and so on. Some marine biologists examine sea animals to be sure the animals are healthy and to find out how to keep them healthy.

An archaeologist is a scientist who searches for, and studies, things made and used by people long ago. Many such things can be found on old sunken ships. Some archaeologists, known as marine archaeologists, spend a great deal of time at sea, searching through the wrecks of ancient ships.

# Books to Read

There are so many fine books about the sea, you're sure to find plenty to enjoy. The books listed here are only a sampling. Your school or public library will have many more.

## Ages 5 to 8

**A First Look at Seals, Sea Lions and Walruses** by Millicent E. Selsam and Joyce Hunt (Walker, 1988)
The authors of this book give you a close look at the specialized bodies of these marine mammals.

**How to Hide an Octopus and Other Sea Creatures** by Ruth Heller (Putnam, 1986)
Try to find the octopus and other sea creatures that are hidden in the ocean world pictures.

**Sharks** by Russell Freedman (Holiday, 1985)
Sharks must swim continuously, or they will sink to the bottom of the ocean. Find out why in this book.

**Where the Waves Break, Life at the Edge of the Sea** by Anita Malnig (Carolrhoda, 1985)
Take this book with you when you go beachcombing to help you identify sea animals and plants.

**The Wonderful World of Seals and Whales** by Sandra Lee Crow (National Geographic Society, 1984)
Beautiful photographs help you learn about the habits of seals and whales and how they live in their underwater world.

**World of a Jellyfish** by David Shale and Jennifer Coldrey (Gareth Stevens, 1986)
Jellyfish are such unusual animals! Find out what makes them so special.

**World of Crabs** by Jennifer Coldrey (Gareth Stevens, 1986)
How crabs feed themselves and how they defend themselves are just two of the topics covered in this book.

## Ages 9 and Up

**All About Whales** by Dorothy Hinshaw Patent (Holiday, 1987)
Did you know that sperm whales sometimes dine on giant squid? Or that humpback whales engage in "bubble feeding"? These facts and others are presented in this book.

**The Dangerous Life of the Sea Horse** by Miriam Schlein (Atheneum, 1986)
What does a sea horse father do that other fathers cannot? Find out the answer to this and other questions in this book.

**Dive to the Coral Reefs** by the New England Aquarium Staff (Crown, 1986)
The authors and photographers who made this book are scientists and divers. They show the formation of coral reefs and the many plants and animals that live there.

**Dolphins and Porpoises** by Dorothy Hinshaw Patent (Holiday, 1987)
People are fascinated by dolphins and porpoises because they are so smart and playful. Learn more about these very special ocean creatures.

**Exploring the Sea: Oceanography Today** by Carvell Hall Blair (Random, 1986)
Do you think that you'd like to study the sea? That's what oceanographers do.

**Homes in the Sea: From the Shore to the Deep** by Jean H. Sibbald (Dillon, 1986)
This book examines many of the animals that inhabit the ocean.

**Land Under the Sea** by Hershell H. and Joan Lowery Nixon (Putnam, 1985)
The authors of this book describe how oceanographers map the bottom of the sea.

**Man-of-War at Sea** by David Shale and Jennifer Coldrey (Gareth Stevens, 1986)
This book tells about the habits and describes the features of the Portuguese man-of-war.

**Monster Seaweeds: The Story of the Giant Kelps** by Mary Daegling (Dillon, 1986)
Kelp, a kind of seaweed, is the largest and fastest growing plant in the ocean. The author also tells us how it is used in the sea and on land.

**Night of Ghosts and Hermits: Nocturnal Life on the Seashore** by Mary Stolz (Harcourt, 1985)
Come along with this author to explore the seashore at night and to learn about the nighttime activities of some creatures that live there.

**Ocean Life** by Rick Morris (EDC Pub., 1983)
This book focuses on the unusual and unexplained side of sea life.

**Oceans** by Martyn Bramwell (Watts, 1984)
Color photographs, drawings, and maps of the four major oceans enhance this book.

**Oceans in Peril** by John C. Fine (Atheneum, 1987)
The author of this book is an authority on one of the earth's most valuable natural resources—water. He shares his ideas about how we can treat our oceans carefully and keep them clean.

**The Sea World Book of Seals and Sea Lions** by Phyllis Roberts Evans (Harcourt, 1986)
Learn about pinnipeds, or "fin-footed" animals, in this interesting book.

**Strange Eating Habits of Sea Creatures** by Jean H. Sibbald (Dillon, 1986)
As the author explains the eating habits of many sea animals, one point comes across loud and clear—sea creatures depend upon each other constantly.

**Whales, the Nomads of the Sea** by Helen Roney Sattler (Lothrop, 1987)
Not only does the author share factual information about whales, but she tells about her personal experiences with them. An illustrated glossary of terms is included. Also, look for **Sharks, the Super Fish** by the same author.

**The World's Oceans** by Cass R. Sandak (Watts, 1987)
Underwater archaeology, which includes the study of ancient sunken ships, is one of many subjects in this fascinating book.

**The World of Sharks** by Andrew Langley (Bookwright, 1988)
Sharks come in over two hundred different shapes and sizes! Learn about some of them in this book.

# New words

Here are some of the words you have met in this book. Many of them may be new to you, but all have something to do with the sea. Next to each word, you'll see how to say the word: **antenna** (an TEHN uh). The part in capital letters is said a little more loudly than the rest of the word. One or two sentences under each word tell what the word means.

**antenna** (an TEHN uh)
An antenna is one of the long, slender feelers on the head of some animals, such as the lobster.

**arthropod** (AHR thruh pahd)
An arthropod is an animal with a jointed body, a shell, and three or more pairs of legs. A shrimp is an arthropod. *See also* **crustacean.**

**astrolabe** (AS truh layb)
An astrolabe is an ancient navigating instrument. Sailors used it to measure the angle between the horizon and the sun or a star in order to find out how far north or south they were. *See also* **quadrant.**

**atmosphere** (AT muh sfihr)
The atmosphere is the air that surrounds the earth.

**billow** (BIHL oh)
A billow is a great, swelling wave.

**breaker** (BRAYK uhr)
A breaker is a wave that breaks into foam as it crashes on the shore.

**chronometer** (kruh NAHM uh tuhr)
A chronometer is a very accurate and sensitive clock used for navigation. It helps sailors find out how far east or west they are.

**coelenterate** (sih LEHN tuh rayt)
A coelenterate is one of a group of sea animals that are largely stomachs with tentacles. *See also* **tentacle.**

**compass** (KUHM puhs)
A compass is a direction-finding instrument used for navigation. It has a magnetic needle that always points to the north.

**course** (kawrs)
The direction in which a ship is going is called the ship's course. A ship that is going in the right direction is said to be "on course."

**crustacean** (kruhs TAY shuhn)
A crustacean is any one of a large group of animals with a hard shell, a jointed body, and no backbone. They live mostly in water. Crabs, lobsters, and shrimp are crustaceans. They are part of a larger class of animals called arthropods. *See also* **arthropod.**

**diatom** (DY uh tahm)
A diatom is any one of many very tiny water plants with a hard shell. Diatoms are a basic part of the food chain of the ocean.

**echinoderm** (ih KY nuh durm)
An echinoderm is any one of a group of small sea animals with a tough skin covered with bumps or thorny points.

**galleon** (GAL ee uhn)
The galleon, a large sailing ship that was designed for fighting, appeared in the 1500's. It had three or four masts, square and triangular sails, three or four decks, and cannons on each side.

**hydrogen** (HY druh juhn)
Hydrogen, a gas without color or odor, combines with oxygen to form water.

**lodestone** (LOHD stohn)
Lodestone, or loadstone, is a hard, black stone that acts like a magnet. Long ago, these stones were used as direction-finding instruments. If an oblong lodestone is hung by a string, or placed on a piece of wood and floated in a bowl of water, it will point north and south.

**log glass** (LAWG glas)
A log glass is a small timing device in which sand trickles from the top part to the bottom part in half a minute. It was used with a log line—a line with equally spaced knots along its length

and a piece of wood (the log) tied to the end. The log was tossed into the water and the line allowed to run out. The number of knots that ran out in half a minute (as timed by the log glass) was the speed of the ship. From this, sailors could work out the distance traveled in a given period of time. The use of a knotted log line led to measuring a ship's speed in units called knots.

**mammal** (MAM uhl)
A mammal is any one of a group of warm-blooded animals that is fed milk from the mother's body and has some hair on its body. Walruses, whales, and dolphins are mammals.

**marine archaeologist**
(muh REEN ahr kee AHL uh jihst)
A marine archaeologist is a person who studies ancient objects found in the sea.

**marine biologist**
(muh REEN by AHL uh jihst)
A marine biologist is a person who studies all of the different kinds of animals and plants that live in the sea.

**marine geologist**
(muh REEN jee AHL uh jihst)
A marine geologist is a person who studies the land beneath the sea.

**mollusk** (MAHL uhsk)
A mollusk is one of a group of animals with a soft body and no backbone. Most have some kind of shell. Octopuses and clams are mollusks.

**navigation** (nav uh GAY shuhn)
Navigation is the art or science of figuring out the position or course of a ship at sea.

**nocturnal** (nahk TUR nuhl)
A nocturnal was an ancient instrument used for finding the time at night by means of the stars.

**oceanographer** (oh shuh NAHG ruh fuhr)
An oceanographer is a person who studies the ocean and marine life. It is not a single science, but a number of basic sciences used together.

**oxygen** (AHK suh juhn)
Oxygen is a gas without color, odor, or taste. It is part of the air you breathe. Most animals and plants cannot live without oxygen. Oxygen combines with hydrogen to form water. *See also* **hydrogen.**

**plankton** (PLANGK tuhn)
Plankton is a huge, drifting mass of tiny plants and animals. It is food for many of the animals of the sea.

**quadrant** (KWAHD ruhnt)
A quadrant is an instrument that was used to measure the angle between the horizon and the sun or a star. It helped sailors find out how far north or south they were. But before long, sailors began to use another instrument, the astrolabe, for the same purpose. *See also* **astrolabe.**

**reptile** (REP tuhl)
A reptile is one of a group of scaly skinned, cold-blooded animals that have a backbone and breathe by means of lungs. Snakes and turtles are reptiles.

**spyglass** (SPY glas)
A spyglass is a small telescope.

**submersible** (suhb MUR suh buhl)
A submersible is a boat or other vessel made for underwater research.

**tentacle** (TEHN tuh kuhl)
A tentacle is a long, slender feeler attached to the head or the mouth of an animal. A jellyfish has tentacles.

**trireme** (TRY reem)
A trireme was an ancient warship. It had three rows of oars, one above the other, on each side of the ship. It also had a mast with a large, square sail. When a trireme went into battle, the sail and mast were taken down and the ship was rowed.

**universal ring dial**
(yoo nuh VUR suhl rihng DY uhl)
A universal ring dial was an ancient instrument much like a sundial. It was used to find the time before there were accurate watches.

# Illustration acknowledgments

The publishers of *Childcraft* gratefully acknowledge the courtesy of the following photographers, agencies, and organizations for illustrations in this volume. When all the illustrations for a sequence of pages are from a single source, the inclusive page numbers are given. In all other instances, the page numbers refer to facing pages, which are considered as a single unit or spread. The words *"(left),"* *"(center),"* *"(top),"* *"(bottom),"* and *"(right)"* indicate position on the spread. All illustrations are the exclusive property of the publishers of *Childcraft* unless names are marked with an asterisk (*).

281

# Index

This index is an alphabetical list of the important things covered in both words and pictures in this book. The index shows you what page or pages each thing is on. For example, if you want to find out what the book tells about a particular subject, such as poisonous fish, look under poisonous fish. You will find a group of words, called an entry, like this: **poisonous fish,** 116-117 *(with pictures).* This entry tells you that you can read about poisonous fish on pages 116-117. The words *with pictures* tell you that there are pictures of poisonous fish on these pages, too. Sometimes, the book only tells you about a thing and does not show a picture. Then the words *with picture* will not be in the entry. It will look like this: **Arctic Ocean,** 30. Sometimes, there is only a picture of a thing in the book. Then the word *picture* will appear after the page number, like this: **auger shell,** 192 *(picture).*